The
HealthNut
Cookbook

The *The* HealthNut
COOKBOOK

**Energize Your Day with Over 100
Easy, Healthy, and Delicious Meals**

Nikole Goncalves

PENGUIN

an imprint of Penguin Canada, a division of Penguin Random House Canada Limited

Canada • USA • UK • Ireland • Australia • New Zealand • India • South Africa • China

First published 2019

www.penguinrandomhouse.ca

LIBRARY AND ARCHIVES CANADA CATALOGUING IN PUBLICATION

Goncalves, Nikole, author
      The HealthNut cookbook : energize your day with over 100 easy,
healthy, and delicious recipes / Nikole Goncalves.

Issued in print and electronic formats.
ISBN 978-0-7352-3568-7 (softcover).—ISBN 978-0-7352-3569-4 (electronic)

      1. Quick and easy cooking. 2. Cooking. 3. Nutrition. 4. Cookbooks. I. Title.

TX833.5.G663 2019   641.5'55   C2018-905426-3
                                                          C2018-905427-1

Cover and interior design by Jennifer Lum
Cover and interior photography by Kyla Zanardi
Food and prop styling by Houston Mausner and Kyla Zanardi

Printed and bound in China

10 9 8 7 6 5 4 3 2 1

Penguin
Random House
PENGUIN CANADA

To my loving mom, who has been one of my biggest inspirations in life and who taught me that food is meant to be enjoyed.

CONTENTS

Introduction

I'm thrilled that you are holding this cookbook in your hands, ready to take on a new, non-restrictive, balanced way of healthy eating. A way of eating that is sustainable, because healthy living isn't a fad diet or trend; it is a lifestyle. I can't wait for you to flip through these pages and eat the delicious, colourful, and drool-worthy recipes I've created just for you.

I wasn't always the green-smoothie-junkie, kale-chomping girl I am today. I did grow up in a pretty healthy-eating Portuguese household. My mom always bought whole wheat bread and 1% milk, and we always had a big salad at the dinner table. But as I got older and started working part-time jobs, partying on the weekends, and staying up all night—like most teenagers—I fell into a health rut.

I would often skip breakfast and run off a large coffee till noon. I was addicted to sugar and sweets, and although I was skinny, I had barely worked out a day in my life. Believe it or not, at one point I was even a smoker! The most unhealthy habit of all, though, was working 24/7. Even while going to college, I was working three part-time jobs and saying yes to everything because I just didn't know how to say no to a good opportunity. Running off adrenaline, and not checking in with myself, quickly ran me right into a brick wall of exhaustion. I realized a change was necessary.

It was a slow process, but I steadily started adopting healthier habits, such as eating breakfast, drinking more water than coffee, joining a running club with my boyfriend, Matt, and of course I quit smoking. I didn't know it at the time, but Matt played a huge role in influencing me to start working out, eating healthy, and enjoying life outside of work. Although I initially started eating better and exercising in order to reduce my stress and heal my anxiety, it had an overwhelmingly positive ripple effect. My brittle nails became stronger, my skin became smoother and brighter, and I just felt happier overall. You could say the proof was in the pudding (healthy Lemon Pie Chia Pudding, that is) because when I started to live a healthier lifestyle, all of the positive changes immediately hooked me onto a new way of life.

Throughout my journey I have experimented with just about every diet there is, from vegetarian, Raw Till 4, gluten-free . . . the list goes on. It took a lot of trial and error for me to find a balance that worked for me and my unique body. I quickly began to realize that the food I ate was largely connected to my emotions, stress levels, and mood. For me, food is a proactive approach to keeping my body running at its best. It's medicine without the scary long list of side effects! And if the saying "you are what you eat" is true, then I would rather be a colourful bowl of salad than a sad plate of greasy fries.

I started my blog *HealthNut Nutrition* to share recipes and cooking tips as I was getting more comfortable in the kitchen. In the beginning, my audience numbered about ten people (a.k.a. my family). It wasn't until Matt—or as he's known on the internet, Mr. Matt—and I moved temporarily to Australia that my YouTube career was born. After a year of binge-watching YouTube videos, I finally got up the courage to hit the record button, talk to a camera, and publish my first video. Since then my audience of ten has grown to hundreds of thousands (and counting!) of "HealthNuts" all over the world. Now when I hit that record button I picture all the amazing, beautiful people I hope to inspire and connect with every week through my videos.

My Food Philosophy

People often assume that in order to be healthy and fit, their diet needs to be restricting. I personally don't believe in counting calories, living behind labels, or feeling guilty about treating myself to a slice of cheesecake. There's a misconception out there that because I drink green smoothies and love my veggies, (a) I must be vegan, and (b) I've probably never eaten a cheeseburger in my life. This couldn't be further from the truth, and I'm going to share all my not-so-secret secrets to creating a healthy and balanced relationship with food.

HealthNut Nutrition is all about eating intuitively and consuming primarily unprocessed foods. You won't find any calorie counting here because food doesn't have to be your enemy! Real food is food that provides your body with the nutrients it needs to improve and sustain both your mental and your physical health.

Nowadays, regardless of how busy I am, I always make time for good food and self-care. I love discovering and playing with new foods and flavours to create my own delicious twists on everyone's classic favourites. But to me, delicious is only part of the equation. The HealthNut in me loves to make sure that every dish I make is balanced in a way that proves healthy eating doesn't have to be tasteless or boring. I live by the 80/20 approach; that means eating healthy 80 percent of the time, while leaving 20 percent for sweets and wine. So if you're looking for recipes that are easy, healthy, and always tasty, you've found the cookbook for you.

My 10 Healthy Habits

One of the most important lessons I've learned over the years is that health should be approached in a holistic way. Health is not just about what you put into your body, how many minutes you work out, or shooting down wheatgrass shots. It's also about the thoughts you think, the people you surround yourself with, connecting with nature, and listening to your body. Over the last few years, I've made self-care a priority in my life and, just like brushing my teeth, I spend time every day doing acts of self-care that support my health. Here are ten healthy habits that have dramatically improved my mental health, mood, relationship with myself, and overall happiness.

1. Listen to Your Body

It seems like every week there's a new diet, food, or exercise regimen trending and, for many of us, it can create a lot of confusion about what it means to be healthy. When it comes to your health, I believe that becoming in tune with how certain foods make you feel can help you find a customized way of eating that fits you and your unique needs. Simply put, eat more of the foods that leave you feeling energized and less of the ones that leave you feeling sluggish. For example, I have learned to avoid caffeine because it triggers my anxiety and gives me excess energy I don't need. Same goes for other common sensitivity foods like dairy, gluten, and soy. Pay attention to how you feel after you eat these foods. Just because everyone else seems to be on the gluten-free bandwagon doesn't mean that it's the right choice for you and that you have to stop eating gluten.

2. Follow Your Stomach

They say your gut is your second brain and that it not only helps you to digest your food but it also can affect your mental health. Ever notice when you feel nervous or anxious, your stomach is the first area you feel it? (Haven't you said "I've got butterflies in my stomach" when you're head over heels for someone or nervous about a job interview?) Since food can affect our mood, I focus on eating foods that I know will digest easily and keep both my blood sugar and mood balanced throughout the day. I also try to listen to my body about what types of foods it is craving, because cravings are often the body's way of letting us know what it's lacking.

3. Recognize That Calories Don't Count

As a self-taught chef and food blogger/YouTuber in the health world, I often get asked for the nutrition data and calorie counts of the recipes I create. Truth is, I have no idea how many calories or grams of healthy fats are in my Almond Swirl Chocolate Brownies, and I'm okay with that. I focus my energy on knowing what ingredients are in my food versus how long it will take to burn them off. One hundred calories from a can of soda will react very differently in the body than 100 calories from broccoli. Instead of worrying about macros and food calculators, I focus on eating wholesome foods that my body will recognize and can easily absorb nutrients from. Besides, math was never my favourite subject in school anyway.

And forget about the concept of "cheat meals," because last time I checked, eating isn't a school exam. If you'd like to eat a cupcake, then eat a cupcake. If you're at a cocktail party, enjoy the appetizers and a glass of wine (or two). In moderation, these foods are fine. The trouble starts when they become daily habits. Trust me, the stress of not eating these "bad foods" is going to do more harm to your body and mind than just treating yourself and enjoying the moment.

4. Sit Quietly and Meditate

Just like going to the gym to exercise your body, it's important to exercise your mind through some kind of meditation that works for you. When I started, I found it extremely difficult to sit quietly even for 5 or 10 minutes—every minute felt like an eternity. After a lot of practice and patience, I have settled on a meditation practice that works for me. It's called self-hypnosis and I do it for 30 minutes a day. This alone has been one of the biggest changes in my life for relieving negative thought patterns, anxiety, and stress. You can find a ton of free guided meditations on YouTube and via apps and podcasts, or you can just sit quietly with or without music. There is no wrong way to meditate, just one that works for you that you can consistently practice.

5. Unplug from the Digital World

As with most people, social media is a huge part of my life, but I've found it extremely important to find time to unplug from the world. This has been a tough one for me, but every night I try setting my phone to airplane mode and placing it in another room. I've also been trying to set aside one day a week (usually Sunday) where I don't go on my phone for most of the day, so I can live mindfully with whomever I'm spending time with—even if that person is just me. You can download apps that track or disable your social media and phone usage to help you cut down. Another great trick I do, when I really need to disconnect, is to delete certain apps like Instagram and Gmail from my phone so I'm not tempted to check them every 5 minutes. The next morning it takes 2 minutes to add them back to my phone. Whichever way you choose to do it, reducing the amount of time you spend online can really increase your mental space and the creativity in your life.

6. Practise Self-Love

Loving yourself and having a positive conversation internally has a big influence on your beliefs, perspective, and attitude towards life. Throughout the day I like to say positive affirmations, such as "I release fears, anxieties, and worries and allow in peace, love, and happiness." I'm usually doing this with sage burning while sitting on a pillow in lotus pose, but that may be too hippy-dippy for some people, so just saying them out loud in the car is perfectly acceptable too. Talking to yourself out loud may feel silly at first, but over time you will notice the difference when you actually start to believe what it is you're telling yourself. Your mind only knows what you tell it, so if you're constantly thinking the same negative thoughts over and over again ("I'm fat," "I'm not good enough," "I'll never find the right partner"), then that is what your mind will believe. Instead, flip those thoughts! Repeat to yourself, "I love my body," "I am enough," "I will meet the right person when I am ready." You'll be amazed at how things start to shift just by changing your perspective.

7. Create Daily Routines

If you follow me on social media or my YouTube channel, then you know I am all about creating routines to help keep me grounded, focused, and calm. Every morning, no matter where I am, I try to start my day by drinking lemon water, spritzing my face with rose water, meditating, and making my bed. Some mornings I add extra things, like a yoga stretch or nature walk, but usually that's on the weekends when I have more free time to play with. Similarly, at night I dim the lights, diffuse essential oils, turn my phone on airplane mode, and make a cup of herbal tea. Doing the same two or three things every morning and night allows your body to recognize it is time to wake up and start the day or wind down and have a restful sleep. Even when I travel I will pack essential oils and my journal and buy fresh lemons once I arrive at my destination, just to ensure I can stick to my routine as much as possible.

8. Practise Gratitude

Practising gratitude shifts your focus away from what you don't have and instead directs it towards the amazing things you do have. For this reason alone, gratitude can help increase your mood and overall well-being and happiness. Every day I write in my journal three things I am grateful for, and this allows me to think about small victories like finishing a new book I'm reading, or about things I take for granted, like my strong legs that get me around. Another reason I enjoy this practice is because it forces me to stop and appreciate the goals I've achieved rather than constantly focusing on my next step. Tomorrow morning when you wake up, reach out your arms for a good body stretch and repeat "I love my life and I am grateful."

9. Get Grounded (Literally)

There is something so grounding and peaceful about spending time in nature. Ever notice how good you feel after a long day at the beach or after a hike in the forest? Although I live in a colder climate and work from home, I make it a priority to get outside every single day and enjoy some good old vitamin D and fresh air. It can be something as simple as walking to do an errand or eating my lunch outside on the balcony. However I do it, being out in nature helps the stress melt away and creates some mental clarity. Next time you are at the park take your shoes and socks off and feel the grass between your toes. Stop by a neighbour's garden and smell the flowers. Or just buy a new plant for your home to bring some nature into your space.

10. Catch Your Z's

They say "no rest for the wicked," so unless you're an evil villain in a Disney movie, get your beauty rest! Sleep to me is just as enjoyable as food—and I love food. Our bodies crave and thrive on consistency, so I make regular, quality sleep a top priority. Everyone is different, but I need seven to eight hours of sleep each night or I feel off the next day. Pick a time to hit the sheets and wake up the next day, and try to stick with that schedule on both weekdays and weekends. Once your body settles into a sleeping pattern, you might even find yourself waking up at the same time each day without the need for an alarm blasting in your ear. Although I don't recommend relying on your body's alarm clock for work or an important exam, on the weekends it can be fun to set your alarm clock 5 or 10 minutes later and see which alarm wakes you up first.

How to Use This Book: Read, Cook, Eat, Repeat!

I hope your taste buds are excited, because they're in for a delicious menu filled with easy and healthy meals. So grab your knife and fork and let's dig in!

The HealthNut Cookbook is designed for those of you who are looking to incorporate quick and easy healthy recipes into your busy schedules. Inside you'll find over one hundred recipes for breakfasts, lunch or dinners (see my "Plates and Bowls" chapter), snacks, and desserts, many of which can be prepared or cooked in 30 minutes or less. Each recipe is made with a combination of plant-based and meat proteins, with easy substitutions for dairy-free and gluten-free options.

Whether you're vegan, gluten-free, paleo, pescatarian, vegetarian, flexitarian, or any other arian, you will find something delicious in these chapters to cook up. My recipes are meant to be mixed, matched, and substituted to fit your lifestyle and diet needs. So whether you're a "certified" HealthNut, don't know the difference between broccoli and kale, or just looking to eat more real, plant-based food, this book is for you.

At the beginning of each recipe, you'll find the prep and cook time to give you a sense of how long the recipe will take to complete. The recipes in this book are meant to be quick and easy to follow and most can be prepared *or* cooked in 30 minutes. Some recipes, such as my Peanut Butter Chocolate Cheesecake (page 208), have an additional chill time listed if they need some extra time to set. That being said, cooking times may vary depending on your oven and stovetop.

Also at the beginning of each recipe, you will find symbols that provide at-a-glance information about dietary accommodations and guidance on recipe prep and planning.

Gluten-Free Recipes that contain no wheat or gluten products. Always check the labels of your packaged foods to make sure they are certified gluten-free, as even products like oats, which do not contain wheat, can be cross-contaminated during processing or packaging.

Plant-Based Vegetarian or vegan recipes filled with lots of plants and containing zero meat.

Meal Prep Friendly Dishes that store well in the fridge or on the counter for several days, making them perfect for your weekly meals and snacks.

Pack and Freeze Dishes that are freezer friendly. These dishes are perfect for bulk cooking and for freezing leftovers for a busy day.

The recipes are organized into these six chapters.

Breakfast Rise and shine, it's breakfast time! Along with brushing my teeth and not working from home in pyjamas all day, my number one priority when I get up is putting together a nourishing meal to start my day on a healthy note. What I eat depends on the day of the week, the time I wake up, and what mood I'm in. I go through phases all the time and will often eat the same thing for a few days in a row before switching to something new and exciting. I love that breakfast is such a versatile meal. You can have something either sweet and dessert-like or a bit more saucy and savoury—there really are no rules. It's a meal so loved that they even made a second version, what we call "brunch." This chapter is filled with everything from my Everyday Gluten-Free Fluffy Pancakes (page 49) to my Good Morning Breakfast Salad (page 45) to give you plenty of ideas for the most important meal of the day.

Nourishing Snacks and Drinks No matter where I am, you will always find me with a drink (usually a water bottle) in one hand and some kind of snack in the other. You might say my purse doubles as my lunch box! As someone who loves food, carrying healthy snacks with me wherever I go is a must. Whether it's for a road trip, a picnic, or game night, snacks and drinks are everything, and I refuse to let anyone go hungry on my watch. From Lemon Herb White Bean Hummus (page 79), Honey-Roasted Sriracha Cashews (page 75), and Pink Lattes (page 98), to my Blueberry Basil Smoothie (page 101), this chapter has got you covered for everything in between breakfast, lunch, and dinner. Say goodbye to hitting up the drive-thru for a midday doughnut.

Salads In my world, there is no wrong way to make a salad. The one thing that does matter, though, is the dressing! The right mix of oils, vinegars, mustard, and spices is what brings a salad to life. Without a decent dressing, you're just eating mixed veggies in a bowl. Every single one of these salads that I've created, like my Fennel Citrus Kale Salad (page 115) or my Beauty Glow Salad (page 128), has its very own mouth-watering homemade dressing. I hope this chapter changes the way you view salads, from something boring to something you actually crave and want to eat every single day. Besides, when salads look and taste this good, you are guaranteed to make friends.

Plates and Bowls For me, lunch and dinner are interchangeable, and this chapter is exactly that. These simple and healthy recipes are sure to answer the never-ending question, "What's for dinner?" You'll find family favourites with a twist, like my Baked Crispy Quinoa Chicken Fingers (page 180), Baked Mac and Cheese, Please (page 159), Quickie Turkey Chili (page 165), and one of my favourites, Mushroom Fettuccine Alfredo (page 155). The best part is that whether you're vegan, paleo, gluten-free, or a devoted carnivore, there is sure to be a recipe that suits your lifestyle and cravings. Use these recipes for your weekend meal prep, quick on-the-go lunch ideas, or just to simply switch up your dinner routine. All are easy to make, all are healthified, and—more importantly—all taste delicious! Go ahead and delete your Uber Eats app because these recipes will reignite your love for cooking in the kitchen and eating good old homemade food.

Sweets Dessert—the sweet course eaten at the end of a meal . . . although I don't think it's a coincidence that the best is saved for last. There is just something so therapeutic about rolling out the perfect dough, scooping cake batter into muffin cups, or swirling almond butter into brownies. Living a healthy lifestyle is not just about the ingredients you use; it's also about connecting with your food. I love baking up fun and healthier options of my childhood favourite desserts because it takes me right back to baking blueberry muffins in the kitchen with Momma HealthNut. The sweet treats in this chapter are made with simple ingredients like eggs, organic butter, spelt flour, and sprinkles (of course!). Bake up a classic, like Fudgy Peanut Butter Cookies (page 187), or try something new, such as my Strawberry Rhubarb Hand Pies (page 196). Whichever route you go, you're in for a treat—pun intended!

HealthNut Staples This is your go-to chapter for the staples I use in my kitchen all the time, like Almond Flour Parm (page 225), Nacho Average Cheese Sauce (page 226), and my drool-worthy Coconut Butter Lemon Glaze (page 232). You'll want to bookmark this chapter because it will be one you'll be coming back to—both for recipes in the book and for your own creations. So go ahead and use these staples to drizzle, sprinkle, spread, and glaze as you please.

Ingredients and Substitutions

Most of the ingredients used in my recipes can easily be found in supermarkets. But just in case you aren't able to find something, here are some substitutions to help you out.

Dairy-free Milk Non-dairy milks are used throughout this cookbook for things like smoothies, baked goods, and pancakes. Look for "unsweetened" on the label to avoid any extra sugar—which, in savoury dishes especially, isn't needed. Some of my favourites are almond milk, coconut milk, organic soy milk, and a recent addition to the list, oat milk. Don't feel you have to use non-dairy milk, though, as these recipes also work with regular cow or sheep milk if you prefer those options. For baking, I like to use organic soy milk, as I find it has a creamy, thicker consistency, and for pancakes and smoothies I usually opt for almond, oat, or coconut milk.

You will notice that two types of coconut milk are used in this book: canned full-fat coconut milk and unsweetened coconut milk from the carton. Make sure you use the one your recipe calls for, because they are very different from each other: the carton version is more watered down and will not firm up in recipes like my Key Lime Pie in a Jar (page 199).

Flours There are so many amazing flours out there, and I'm always experimenting. My recipes call for some staple flours I use all the time, as well as a few that come in handy once in a while, such as chickpea flour. Although I am not gluten intolerant, I do tend to consume low-gluten flours for easy digestion. My all-purpose flours are brown rice and spelt, and these are the ones used the most throughout the book. I am not the biggest fan of gluten-free blends that involve five different flours combined, so instead I opt for using just one or two flours in a recipe to keep things super simple.

You'll also notice that both regular spelt flour and light spelt flour are called for in different recipes. That is because they have a different flavour and texture, but they are pretty much interchangeable. Some flours can be replaced with others, such as whole wheat for spelt, but others, such as coconut flour and chickpea flour, cannot. Substituting flours that have different absorbency will require additional changes, such as less or more flour or liquid, to make them work in a recipe.

Several of my recipes call for almond flour. Just a heads up that almond flour and almond meal may seem similar, but there are minor differences. Both are essentially ground almonds, although almond flour is blanched almonds (skins removed) with a finer texture. Almond meal, on the other hand, can be blanched or unblanched almonds (with or without skins) with a coarser texture. Although they can be used interchangeably, I prefer almond flour in most of my recipes for its consistency and colour.

Fats and Oils Like flours, many different butters and oils can be used for cooking and baking. In this book you'll see avocado oil used in high-temperature cooking because it has a higher smoke point and therefore won't burn as quickly. It can be swapped out for grapeseed or coconut oil. For sautéing and a more buttery flavour, I use ghee, a clarified butter that can be replaced with regular organic unsalted butter. And of course there is the popular extra-virgin olive oil, which I use a lot throughout this book, in salad dressings and for sautéing, as it adds a lot of flavour to a dish.

As for coconut oil, there are two kinds you can use, depending on the flavour you prefer. If you're not a huge fan of coconut flavour in your food, use the refined oil, which has been processed so the coconut flavour is much less detectable than in the unrefined, cold-pressed oil. Coconut butter, also known as "coconut manna," is sometimes confused with coconut oil, but it is actually the meat and oil of the coconut mixed together. I use this in my Coconut Butter Lemon Glaze (page 232) for a creamy, smooth texture, but it is also great drizzled on pancakes.

Sweeteners You will find no cane sugar, corn syrup, or any other refined processed sugars in this book. I use natural sugars such as maple syrup, honey, coconut sugar, blackstrap molasses, and brown rice syrup. Unlike refined sugars, natural sugars contain vitamins, minerals, and fibre and tend to have a lower glycemic index value, which means they won't raise the blood sugar as much. If you're vegan, swap the honey for maple syrup for similar results. The desired consistency or flavour of a dish determines the type of sweetener I use. For instance, brown rice syrup provides a chewy texture in my Salted Caramel Stovetop Granola (page 41).

Spices How much heat you add to your dish is completely up to you. I've listed the amount I prefer to use in each recipe, but feel free to adjust based on your preference. In recipes where I say to use fresh cayenne chili peppers—which are the long, skinny red chilis—you can replace them with ground cayenne pepper or red chili flakes. When you're cooking, start with a little and add as needed. You will also notice I like to use sambal oelek, which is my favourite chili paste and goes well in a lot of Asian-inspired recipes, like peanut sauce and stir-fries, but you can also use Sriracha.

Kitchen Staples

Keeping my fridge and pantry stocked with my go-to staples and fresh ingredients is essential so I always have the ingredients I need to whip up healthy meals. Over the years I've tasted and played around with loads of "magical" superfoods, spices, and vegetables with odd-sounding names. When it comes down to it, I like to stick to my tried-and-true basics while including a fun addition here and there (like nutritional yeast, which may sound odd, but I promise it's delicious). To help you shop for the ingredients used in this book, I've listed all of them below. Once you have your kitchen stocked, you'll be ready to cook up a food storm.

What's in My Pantry?

Condiments and Sauces

- Dill pickles
- Grainy Dijon mustard
- Kimchi
- Mayonnaise
- Sambal oelek chili paste
- Sriracha
- Sun-dried tomatoes
- Gluten-free tamari
- Toasted sesame oil
- White miso paste

Oils and Vinegars

- Avocado oil
- Coconut oil
- Extra-virgin olive oil
- Apple cider vinegar
- Red wine vinegar
- Rice vinegar
- White wine vinegar

Grains and Flours

- Almond flour
- Arrowroot flour
- Chickpea flour
- Coconut flour
- Oat flour
- Spelt flour (light and regular)
- Bread (tortilla wraps, buns, rye, sourdough)
- Brown rice pasta (fettuccine, shells, macaroni, ramen, soba)
- Gluten-free rice bread crumbs
- Old-fashioned rolled oats
- Quinoa (white and red)
- Rice-paper wrappers
- Tortilla corn chips

Baking

- Baking powder
- Baking soda
- Cacao powder
- Unsweetened applesauce
- Semi-sweet chocolate chips
- Semi-sweet baking chocolate
- Sprinkles (with no artificial colours)

Sweeteners

- Blackstrap molasses
- Brown rice syrup
- Coconut sugar
- Pure liquid honey
- Pure maple syrup

Dry Goods and Canned Foods

- Black beans
- Black-eyed peas
- Chickpeas (canned and dried)
- Cannellini beans (white kidney beans)
- Red kidney beans
- Navy beans
- Refried black beans
- Capers
- Canned diced tomatoes
- Canned full-fat coconut milk
- Popcorn kernels
- Pumpkin purée
- Sushi rice
- Tomato paste

Herbs, Spices, and Extracts

- Black pepper (ground and whole)
- Cardamom
- Cayenne pepper
- Chipotle chili powder
- Cinnamon (ground and stick)
- Curry powder
- Dried bay leaves
- Dried dill
- Dried oregano
- Dried parsley
- Dried rosemary
- Dried thyme
- Fennel seeds
- Garam masala
- Garlic powder
- Ground allspice
- Ground coriander
- Ground cumin
- Ground ginger
- Ground nutmeg
- Ground sage
- Ground turmeric
- Italian seasoning
- Old Bay seasoning
- Onion powder
- Sea salt
- Sweet paprika
- Smoked sweet paprika
- Sumac
- Red chili flakes
- Za'atar
- Almond extract
- Peppermint extract
- Pure vanilla extract

Seeds, Nuts, and Dried Fruit

- Chia seeds (whole and ground)
- Flaxseeds (ground and whole)
- Hemp hearts
- Peanuts (salted roasted and redskin)
- Pine nuts
- Raw almonds
- Raw cashews
- Raw pecans
- Raw pumpkin seeds
- Raw sunflower seeds
- Raw walnuts
- Sesame seeds
- Sliced almonds
- Dried fruit
- Dried cranberries
- Medjool dates
- Thompson raisins
- Unsweetened shredded coconut

Specialty Items

- Citric acid (optional)
- Grass-fed collagen powder
- Hawaiian spirulina powder
- Herbal coffee
- Low sodium chicken stock
- Low sodium vegetable stock
- Medium salsa
- Nutritional yeast
- Vanilla plant-based protein powder
- Vegetable bouillon cubes

What's in My Fridge?

Fruits

- Apples (red and green)
- Bananas (fresh and frozen)
- Blackberries
- Blueberries (fresh and frozen)
- Cherries (fresh and frozen)
- Lemons
- Limes
- Mango (frozen)
- Oranges
- Peaches (frozen)
- Pomegranate
- Pineapple (fresh and frozen)
- Raspberries (fresh and frozen)
- Strawberries (fresh and frozen)
- Watermelon

Vegetables

- Alfalfa sprouts
- Asparagus
- Avocado
- Bok choy (baby and Shanghai)
- Baby spinach
- Bean sprouts
- Beets
- Broccoli (regular and Chinese)
- Butter lettuce
- Brussels sprouts
- Carrots
- Cayenne chili pepper
- Cauliflower
- Celery
- Corn kernels (fresh and frozen)
- English cucumber
- Fennel
- French green beans
- Garlic
- Green onions
- Ginger
- Jalapeño peppers
- Kale (curly and black)
- Leeks
- Mushrooms (button, shimeji, cremini, shiitake, king oyster, portobello)
- Olives (black and Kalamata)
- Onions (yellow and red)
- Peas (fresh and frozen)
- Poblano peppers
- Peperoncini peppers (pickled)
- Potatoes (mini red and mini yellow Yukon Gold)
- Shallots
- Spring pea microgreens
- Spring mixed greens
- Squash (acorn and butternut)
- Sweet potatoes
- Sweet red pepper
- Swiss chard
- Radishes
- Red cabbage
- Romaine lettuce
- Rhubarb
- Tomatoes (cherry, heirloom, vine)
- Turmeric root
- Zucchini (green and yellow)

Fresh Herbs

- Basil
- Chives
- Cilantro
- Mint
- Parsley (flat-leaf and curly)
- Rosemary
- Thyme

Nut and Seed Butters

- Natural almond butter
- Natural cashew butter
- Natural coconut butter
- Natural peanut butter
- Tahini

Dairy and Dairy-free Alternatives

- Feta cheese
- Halloumi cheese
- Soft goat cheese
- Plain full-fat coconut yogurt
- Plain full-fat Greek and regular yogurt
- Ghee
- Organic unsalted butter
- Unsweetened coconut milk
- Unsweetened almond milk
- Unsweetened soy milk

Meat, Seafood, Eggs, and Other Protein

- Thick-cut bacon
- Boneless, skinless chicken breasts
- Organic free-run eggs
- Lean ground pork
- Lean ground turkey
- Smoked salmon
- Wild salmon fillets
- Extra-firm organic tofu

Equipment

There are some great cooking equipment staples every home cook should have in their kitchen. But, don't feel like you need to run to the store or scroll through Amazon to purchase everything all at once. Take time building up your kitchen and finding the tools that work for you (and look for sales)! I've listed my most used and loved kitchen accessories below. If you want direct links to the exact brands I use, you can head to www.healthnutnutrition.ca/equipment for a full list with links.

Small Appliances
- Food processor
- Hand-held electric mixer
- High-speed blender
- Waffle maker

Cutting
- Wood and plastic cutting boards
- Chef's knife
- Ceramic knives
- Microplane zester
- Vegetable peeler
- Grater
- Mandoline slicer
- Spiralizer

Measuring
- Measuring spoons
- Dry and liquid measuring cups

Baking
- Baking sheets
- Muffin tin
- Doughnut pan
- 8-inch square baking pan
- 4-inch round tart pans
- 9- x 5-inch loaf pan
- Cooling racks
- Silicone baking mats
- Muffin liners

Utensils
- Rubber spatulas
- Whisk
- Tongs
- Pizza cutter
- Citrus juicer
- Ice-cream scoops

Storage
- Mixing bowls
- Glass jars
- Airtight glass containers
- Resealable freezer bags

Pots and Pans

- Cast-iron skillet
- Non-stick skillets (with lids) and saucepans
- Large soup pot
- Steamer basket

Other

- Fine-mesh strainer
- Colander
- Rolling pin
- Glass straws
- Food scale

MEAL PREP
101

I never used to think meal prepping for the week was something I would ever enjoy doing, because I love variety and being creative in the kitchen. Thankfully I discovered that Sunday night meal prepping can be a lot of fun once I customized it to fit my lifestyle and taste buds. There is no one-size-fits-all approach! Why meal prep at all, you ask? I know so many people who are more than happy to eat rice, chicken, and steamed veggies every single night of the week because for them, food is simply fuel for the body. But if you're a foodie/HealthNut like me, then you know that food is something much more than just nourishment—it's an experience! I often find myself daydreaming about what I'm going to make for dinner, what I'll have for breakfast later in the week, or what I should bake on the weekend. I need to feel excited about sitting down to each meal so I can savour and really enjoy what I'm putting into my body (hence me being the slowest eater alive, but hey, it's great for digestion, so I'm not complaining). Variety is what keeps me motivated to eat healthy, wholesome foods. Want to join in on the deliciousness? Here are some meal-prep tips and an action plan to get you started on your journey to becoming a meal prepping queen or king in the kitchen!

Benefits of Meal Prep

I often get asked what my secret is to maintaining a healthy diet and lifestyle while running a full-time business. My answer? You guessed it: meal prepping! It doesn't matter if you're Beyoncé, Elon Musk, or the president of the United States, everyone has 24 hours in a day—and the only way to get more free time is to become more efficient with what you do.

Setting aside time each week for planning my meals not only keeps me on track with my health goals but also means I spend less time in the kitchen throughout the week, which in turn means more time for hobbies and relaxation, like spending time with family or going to a yoga class. It also means spending less money on takeout, and using that money instead for other things in life, such as travel, special occasions, or that

new pair of runners I've been eyeing for weeks. Not to mention that by meal prepping, you'll more likely be able to avoid those inconvenient "hangry" moments. Like most people, I'm no fun to be around when I'm hungry. For that reason, I always keep a stash of made-ahead Oatmeal Raisin Cookie Energy Bites (page 94), Salted Caramel Stovetop Granola (page 41), or good old fresh fruit in my bag to avoid having to buy junkier foods on the go.

How to Get Started

As a beginner, there are a few things you'll need to do to get you and your kitchen prepared so that each week runs as smoothly as possible. Once you have a system in place, you'll become faster at meal prepping.

The first thing you'll need to do is clean out and organize your fridge and pantry. Get a good idea of what ingredients you currently have, and ensure you've got enough space to store containers of your cooked/prepared food. Next, stock up on food storage containers in different shapes and sizes. I prefer using glass and plastic containers that are BPA-free or made from recycled material. Wide-mouth glass jars are great for storing dressings, soups, bircher muesli, and chia puddings. Other supplies you might want to stock up on are silicone storage bags (I personally love the ones by Stasher Bags), silicone baking mats, and cooking tools like measuring cups, knives, a food processor, and a blender. Once you have your space prepared and your supplies on hand, you're ready to get started! You can find a list of my favourite kitchen equipment on page 15 as a reference.

Create an Action Plan Take it from someone who always wants to skip step 1 and jump to step 3, sitting down to plan out a meal-prep template is crucial to making meal prep a habit and not a one-week trend like that sequin bomber jacket you bought last spring.

Create a Schedule Schedule a day and time in your week, just like an appointment, to set aside for meal prep.

Set a Budget You'll need to set a budget for how much you want to spend each week, so you can be on the lookout for sales and have a better idea of which stores to go to. You might also opt for cheaper cuts of meat or only buy organic produce if it's among the Dirty Dozen, which is a list of fruits and vegetables with the highest loads of pesticide residue. Usually foods with thin skin (such as berries, leafy greens, and apples) and root vegetables that are grown directly in the soil (like potatoes, carrots, and turnips) are best bought organic. The Dirty Dozen (2018) includes:

- Strawberries
- Spinach
- Nectarines
- Apples
- Grapes
- Peaches
- Cherries
- Pears
- Tomatoes
- Celery
- Potatoes
- Sweet bell peppers

The flipside of the Dirty Dozen is the Clean Fifteen—a list of produce with the least amount of pesticide residue. Buying these organic is not as important if beyond your budget. The Clean Fifteen (2018) includes:

- Avocados
- Sweet corn
- Pineapples
- Cabbages
- Onions
- Sweet peas (frozen)
- Papayas
- Asparagus
- Mangoes
- Eggplants
- Honeydew melons
- Kiwis
- Cantaloupe
- Cauliflower
- Broccoli

Choose Your Recipes Decide which recipes you're in the mood for that week, based on the time of year, the weather (is it barbecue season or cuddle-up-under-a-blanket season?), how busy you are, and what's in season and local. You can also schedule themed dinner nights, like Meatless Mondays or Taco Tuesdays, which helps to narrow down the recipe possibilities.

Get Inspired Browse through Instagram, Pinterest (a foodie's heaven), YouTube, food blogs and magazines, and of course good old cookbooks (cough cough, like the one you're holding!). Bookmark these recipes or print them out to have them ready for when you're making your grocery list.

Share the Love If you live with others, take turns cooking or get the whole family involved. You can have someone chopping veggies while you're stirring the soup pot so you can prepare for the week in half the time while also having some good company. If you're prepping by yourself (which can be very therapeutic!), pop on a good podcast or Spotify playlist to make the time fly by.

Shop Like a Pro Sitting down to create your shopping list is almost as important as the cooking process. If you don't make a list, you'll either forget a bunch of necessary ingredients or impulse shop and end up with things you don't need—which is never good for the wallet. Speaking of wallets, be sure to stay within your budget to avoid overspending. Shop at discount stores, buy staples in bulk, and price-match through flyers or apps. Switch up your ingredients or brands by taking advantage of what's on sale and what's in season and local. A lot of ingredients are interchangeable in cooking, so I always look out for what's on sale and stock up on basics.

I keep an ongoing grocery list attached to the front of my fridge that lists all my kitchen staples so I can simply check off the items I need as I run low. That way, when the time comes to grocery shop, I already know which basics I need to stock up on. It's one less thing I need to remember! I've done the work for you and created a shopping list template that you can print out, laminate, and stick on your fridge. You can download your template at www.healthnutnutrition.ca/shoppingtemplate.

Prep and Cook

You've written up your meal plan for the week, gone shopping, and now you're ready to prep! There are many different ways to meal prep. Choosing which way works for you depends on your lifestyle and eating habits.

Option 1: Standard Meal Prep A basic option is to cook a large batch of individual meals for breakfast, lunch, dinner, and snacks all week long. For example, if you chose to have chia pudding for breakfast, you would make enough for all 5 or 7 days of the week (depending on if you want to meal prep for weekends too). Or you would portion out your meat, veggies, and grains into containers ready for lunches and dinners each day of the week. This method can work for those of you who enjoy routine and don't mind eating the same thing for a week straight. My boyfriend, Matt, is a great example of this as he loves to know he has meals prepped and ready to grab from the fridge and is happy to eat the same thing for a few days in a row.

Option 2: Buffet Style Another option is to cook up large batches of individual whole foods. For example, a large batch of quinoa, roasted veggies, a whole roasted chicken, chopped kale, and so on. It's like your own personal buffet in your fridge. When the time comes to whip up a meal, simply look at what you've prepped and pull it together into a yummy, nourishing meal. Perhaps make a nourish bowl, a quick soup, or a burrito. Since you have all the ingredients precooked and chopped, you can be sitting down to eat in no time.

Option 3: The Hybrid I prefer a hybrid method of the two, where I batch cook both individual ingredients and whole meals to have throughout the week. This way I have the option of either heating up a precooked meal or throwing together something fast like a stir-fry on a night when I get home late and I'm too tired to cook. Sometimes I prep individual items like beans and grains just to add to other recipes I'll be cooking to speed up the process, and sometimes I can put a few of those together to make a complete meal. Get creative! Use your cooked quinoa not only as a side but also as a base for curry or mixed into your morning bowl of oats for some extra protein. Here is an example of a Hybrid Meal Prep Week:

- Rise and Shine Breakfast Cookies (page 31)
- Chickpea Curry in a Hurry (page 160)
- Baked Crispy Quinoa Chicken Fingers (page 180)
- Fluffy Cooked Quinoa (page 219)
- Raw spiralized zucchini
- Raw chopped kale (for adding to smoothies or salads)
- Jammy Eggs (page 218)
- Beet Goat Cheese Hummus (page 80)
- Steamed and Frozen Cauliflower Florets for smoothies (see page 223)
- Chewy Trail Mix Granola Bars (page 92)

Meal Prep Tips and Hacks

You can prep all kinds of things ahead of time to make cooking throughout the week that much quicker. For instance, if you know you're going to have fresh lemon juice and warm water each morning, squeeze a few fresh lemons into a glass jar, screw on the lid, and refrigerate. I also like to store peeled and chopped garlic and onions in the fridge to add to meals like stir-fries, soups, and chilis. Essentially any ingredient you know you will be using frequently throughout the week can be prepped all at once.

To help you both visualize and tackle your meal-prepping session, here's a basic guide that breaks down the steps to take and what foods you should start on first.

Preheat the oven to cooking temperature.

Wash and chop your veggies while the oven is preheating—both those you plan to cook now and those you'll be storing raw. Raw veggies like kale, cucumber, sweet peppers, radishes, and celery are perfect to prep in advance, as they won't quickly get soggy or wilted.

Boil water for cooking beans, Jammy Eggs (page 218), or grains. You can also use a rice cooker for an easy "set it and forget it" option for grains like rice and quinoa.

Roast your veggies and proteins in the oven with avocado oil and seasonings.

Blend nut butters, nut milks, dips, and sauces like Beet Goat Cheese Hummus (page 80) and Nacho Average Cheese Sauce (page 226) to have on hand throughout the week for snacks, smoothies, and lattes.

Steam and freeze veggies like butternut squash and cauliflower (see page 223) for smoothies. I usually have one or two batches of bananas ripening in my fruit bowl, ready to peel and freeze for smoothies, oatmeal, and banana bread.

Bake muffins, cookies, or other baked goods once your meat and veggies are roasted and the oven is still hot.

Soak any nuts or seeds you may need for the week, like raw cashews for sauces and salad dressings.

Fill smoothie freezer packs for making smoothies during the week. Fill resealable freezer bags with the solid smoothie ingredients. In the mornings, empty a smoothie pack into your blender, add liquid, and blend.

Four-Week Meal Plan

WEEK ONE
Breakfast Rise and Shine Breakfast Cookies (page 31) + Everyday Green Smoothie (page 107)
Lunch Chickpea Curry in a Hurry (page 160)
Snack Cheesy Dill Popcorn (page 85)
Dinner Saucy Cashew Chicken Lettuce Cups (page 179) + Green Bean Salad with Grated Beet (page 116)
Dessert Lemon Pie Chia Pudding (page 207)

WEEK TWO
Breakfast Strawberry Banana Chia Breakfast Jar (page 42) + Salted Caramel Stovetop Granola (page 41)
Lunch Smoky White Bean Kale Soup (page 162) + Rosemary and Sea Salt Almond Crackers (page 88)
Snack Beet Goat Cheese Hummus (page 80)
Dinner Falafel Mediterranean Bowl (page 148)
Dessert One-Bowl Carrot Cake Muffins (page 192)

WEEK THREE
Breakfast Almond Orange Quinoa Oatmeal (page 33)
Lunch Nutty Noodle Summer Rolls (page 119)
Snack Honey-Roasted Sriracha Cashews (page 75)
Dinner Southwest Black-Eyed Pea Burgers (page 145)
Dessert Fudgy Peanut Butter Cookies (page 187)

WEEK FOUR
Breakfast Everyday Nut and Seed Loaf (page 91) + Blueberry Basil Smoothie (page 101)
Lunch Rainbow Chopped Salad (page 118) + Baked Crispy Quinoa Chicken Fingers (page 180)
Snack Chewy Trail Mix Granola Bars (page 92)
Dinner Roasted Poblano and Mushroom Fajitas (page 176)
Dessert Raw Chocolate Chip Cookie Dough Bites (page 189)

Meal Prep FAQs

1. How long does prepped food last?
Plant-based foods like fruits, veggies, hummus, and cooked beans should keep for up to 5 days. For meals containing animal products such as chicken and fish, I recommend storing 3 days' worth of meals in the fridge and freezing the rest. It's always best to under-prep and have to cook more than to over-prep and be forced to throw out food.

2. How do I store prepared food properly?
I like to store my prepped food in clear containers so I can easily see what's inside without opening up every container. Before storing any hot cooked food, you'll

want to let it cool slightly before transferring to the fridge or freezer. When freezing food, be sure to use sealed airtight containers to prevent air from seeping in and creating freezer burn. Although freezer-burnt food is still edible, it won't taste good! To ensure your meals are kept fresh, your refrigerator should be set between 0 and 4°C (32 and 40°F), and the freezer below 0°C (32°F).

3. How much food should I cook?

The amount of food you prep and cook depends on a number of things, such as how many people live in your household, your schedule, and how big an appetite you have. As you get started with meal prepping, you'll quickly realize whether you're under- or over-prepping and can make adjustments each week to better suit your eating needs and lifestyle. I personally like to prep for 3 to 5 days a week, which gives me some wiggle room for eating out or trying out a new recipe. Remember, meal prepping isn't about limiting or restricting food. It's about being prepared so you have healthy, wholesome food at your fingertips.

4. How should I reheat meals?

I avoid microwaves whenever possible, but I know for many people that's the only option in the lunchroom. If the microwave is your last resort, I suggest reheating your food in a microwave-safe glass container, with the lid popped open, for 2 to 3 minutes, depending on the dish, and stopping to stir it halfway through. If you are planning to enjoy one of your freezer meals the next day, place it in the fridge the night before so it's thawed and ready to be reheated at lunch or dinner. If you have a stovetop available to you, heat up meals using a hot pan with a spray of coconut oil or some water. Add the food, cover, and cook for a few minutes until heated through.

If you're heating up something that you want to stay crispy, like my Baked Crispy Quinoa Chicken Fingers (page 180), pop it on a baking sheet and broil in the oven for a couple of minutes, flipping halfway through. A little hack for heating up things like Zucchini Corn Fritters (page 172) or Everyday Gluten-Free Fluffy Pancakes (page 49) is to pop them into the toaster until they crisp up around the edges. If you've frozen baked goods, you can transfer them straight from your freezer to your lunch box, and by lunch they will be thawed and ready to enjoy.

5. Are there any foods that shouldn't be reheated?

Yes, there are some foods that don't reheat well and should instead be eaten cold or avoided for meal prepping. I find gluten-free pasta does not heat up well (except in casseroles) the next day, so I usually cook just enough for the one day. Keep your pasta sauces separate so you can store any leftovers for a later date.

Cooked and chilled fish and seafood should be eaten cold. (It's delicious on top of a salad.) Eggs are another food that are best eaten cold or at room temperature once they're cooked and refrigerated. Boiled eggs can keep in the fridge for a few days and are perfect sliced onto avocado toast, breakfast burritos, or eaten as is with some salt and pepper.

6. What types of foods and recipes are best for meal prepping?

When it comes to prepping food in advance, there are definitely some ingredients that hold up better than others.

Good for meal prepping: For salads, I look for hearty greens like kale, cabbage, green beans, and broccoli that hold a crunch and won't wilt or get soggy with dressing. Options like my Green Bean Salad with Grated Beet (page 116) or my Shredded Caesar Salad (page 124) will hold up well for a few days in the fridge. Grains and beans are always a safe bet, as well as roasted root veggies like sweet potato, carrots, beets, and turnip. For protein, hard-boiled eggs keep well, and you can leave them unpeeled and put them back in the egg carton for easy storage. As well, any dishes that get better with time (think chilis, soups, stews) are great meal-prep options.

Most baked desserts and snacks, like my Lemon-Glazed Blueberry Muffins (page 190) and Oatmeal Raisin Cookie Energy Bites (page 189), freeze well, so you can make double the batch and freeze them to enjoy over the next month.

Not good for meal prepping: Try to stay away from seafood, watery veggies and fruit, and soft leafy greens if you're prepping your salads ahead of time.

7. How long does it take to meal prep?

The amount of time meal prepping for a week takes varies greatly depending on the types and quantity of meals you're cooking. Generally I block 2 to 3 hours for meal prep, but you may need more or less time. You will get into a groove once you get started and become familiar with some of your go-to meal-prep dishes. If you find it hard to set aside that much time for meal prep, you can do half of it on the weekend and the other half mid-week to break it up.

8. How can I speed up meal prep?

Use small appliances in your kitchen to multitask and speed things up. Slow cookers and rice cookers look after cooking one thing while you're prepping and cooking something else on your stovetop and in the oven. Cook several dishes at the same time in the oven—for example, roast your veggies on one shelf and your meat or fish on another one. If you're going to need a lot of shredded or chopped veggies, use your food processor to prep veggies in seconds, with little cleanup and safe fingers. Lastly, try to stagger your cooking times so you can wash dishes as you go along, which means less cleanup when you're finished.

BREAKFAST

Rise and Shine Breakfast Cookies

Makes 12 to 14 cookies • Prep Time 10 minutes • Cook Time 25 minutes

Ingredients

1 ripe medium banana

2 eggs, lightly beaten

¼ cup natural peanut butter

¼ cup coconut oil, melted

¼ cup unsweetened applesauce

¼ cup pure maple syrup

1 teaspoon pure vanilla extract

1¾ cups old-fashioned rolled oats

1 cup almond flour

½ cup oat flour

¼ unsweetened shredded coconut

1 teaspoon cinnamon

1 teaspoon baking powder

½ teaspoon baking soda

¼ teaspoon sea salt

¼ teaspoon ground nutmeg

¾ cup peeled and grated carrots

½ cup grated apple (Fuji or
Pink Lady)

½ cup Thompson raisins

These cookies are full of all my breakfast favourites—banana, peanut butter, oats, and a side of hidden veggies. I love baking a batch during my Sunday meal prep so they're ready to grab and go all week long. Each cookie is packed with healthy fats, fibre, spice, and everything nice. Whoever said you can't have cookies for a healthy breakfast just hasn't made these! Enjoy warm with a tall glass of Chai Cashew Milk (page 100).

1. Preheat the oven to 350°F. Line a baking sheet with parchment paper.

2. In a medium bowl, mash the banana with a fork. Stir in the eggs, peanut butter, melted coconut oil, applesauce, maple syrup, and vanilla until well combined.

3. In a large bowl, combine the oats, almond flour, oat flour, coconut, cinnamon, baking powder, baking soda, salt, and nutmeg. Stir well.

4. Stir the banana mixture into the flour mixture to combine. Then fold in the carrots, apples, and raisins until well combined.

5. Roll a heaping ¼ cup of batter at a time into balls. Place the balls about 1 inch apart on the prepared baking sheet.

6. Bake the cookies until golden brown on the bottom, 20 to 25 minutes. Let the cookies cool on the baking sheet for 5 minutes before transferring to a rack. Store in an airtight container at room temperature for up to 5 days (that is, if they last that long!).

VARIATION Switch up the carrot for shredded zucchini or sweet potato for a fun twist.

Apple Bircher Muesli

Serves 2 • Prep Time 5 minutes • Chill Time overnight in the fridge

Ingredients

1 cup old-fashioned rolled oats

2 tablespoons chopped raw hazelnuts

2 tablespoons raw sunflower seeds

2 tablespoons chia seeds

2 tablespoons unsweetened shredded coconut or coconut chips

2 tablespoons Thompson raisins

2 Medjool dates, pitted and chopped

¼ teaspoon cinnamon

1 Granny Smith apple, shredded

1½ cups unsweetened almond milk or coconut milk (from the carton)

2 tablespoons fresh orange juice

Toppings (optional)

Fresh raspberries or blueberries

Pure liquid honey

The original overnight oats, bircher muesli! I started making a version of this muesli while living in Australia with my boyfriend, Matt. This amazing grab-and-go breakfast kept me full until lunch and didn't require heating up the stove. (When you're living without air conditioning, that's always a bonus!) Customize it by adding your favourite dried fruits, nuts, and seeds, and it will always come out tasting delicious.

1. In a small bowl, combine the oats, hazelnuts, sunflower seeds, chia seeds, coconut, raisins, dates, and cinnamon. Give it a good stir. Add the shredded apple, almond milk, and orange juice and stir until well combined.

2. Divide the mixture between two 8-ounce glass jars or airtight containers, cover, and refrigerate overnight to soak the oats. Enjoy the next morning with fresh berries and honey, if using. The muesli will store well in the fridge for up to 4 days.

🌰 **HEALTHNUT TIP** If you forget to prep your oats the night before, just mix it up first thing in the morning with quick-cooking oats instead. Let it soak for 30 minutes while you're getting ready for the day ahead.

Almond Orange Quinoa Oatmeal

Serves 2 • **Prep Time 5 minutes** • **Cook Time 25 minutes**

....

Prep Ahead

Vanilla Roasted Almond Butter
(page 228)

Ingredients

2 cups water

Sea salt

¾ cup old-fashioned rolled oats

2 tablespoons red quinoa

½ ripe banana, mashed

Zest of 1 orange

¼ cup unsweetened almond milk or
coconut milk (from the carton)

½ teaspoon cinnamon

Ground nutmeg

¼ teaspoon pure almond extract

Toppings

½ orange, peeled and divided
into segments

2 tablespoons Vanilla Roasted
Almond Butter

2 to 4 tablespoons toasted unsalted
sliced blanched almonds

2 teaspoons pure maple syrup

2 tablespoons unsweetened
coconut milk (from the carton;
optional)

Let's be real: oatmeal by itself is not that exciting. What is exciting is the endless ways you can flavour and top it. Toppings are what bring a bowl of hot oats to life! It took me until my early twenties to discover the wonders of adding mashed banana (compliments of Momma HealthNut). Banana brings the perfect amount of sweetness and makes me feel like I'm eating dessert for breakfast! I can't get enough of this almond orange version, with its pop of red quinoa for crunch. Give it a try—I just know you'll love it!

1. In a medium saucepan, bring the water to a boil with a pinch of sea salt. Stir in the oats and quinoa and reduce the heat to low. Cover and simmer, stirring occasionally, for 12 to 15 minutes, until the water is mostly absorbed and the oats are tender.

2. Add the banana (I like to mash it right in the pot), orange zest, almond milk, cinnamon, a pinch of nutmeg, and almond extract. Stir, cover, and cook for another 5 minutes. Remove from the heat and let the oatmeal sit for another 5 minutes to thicken up.

3. Divide the oatmeal between 2 bowls. Top with orange segments, Vanilla Roasted Almond Butter, and sliced almonds, and drizzle with maple syrup. Top with the coconut milk for a creamier texture, if you like.

VARIATION When it comes to oatmeal, anything goes. You can easily switch out the toppings for berries, use any nut butter of your choice, and add sprinkles of coconut flakes or pumpkin seeds. The world is your bowl of oatmeal.

HEALTHNUT TIP In oatmeal, I like using red quinoa rather than white because I find it retains a heartier texture when cooked for a longer time.

Instant Oatmeal Jars Five Ways

Serves 1 • Prep Time 10 to 15 minutes

Even though I wasn't the biggest oatmeal fan when I was growing up, I really enjoyed instant oatmeal packets (which, let's be honest, were basically brown sugar and tiny pieces of dried apple). Hey, they were quick and tasted like dessert! But thankfully I've discovered a healthier alternative. These DIY oatmeal variations start with a simple and nourishing base of rolled oats and chia seeds, with a secret ingredient of oat flour to give that creamy consistency you loved as a kid. The rest is up to you! Add your favourite sweetener, fruits, nuts, and spices, let it sit for 5 minutes, and you're ready to run out the door with your breakfast in one hand.

Instant Oatmeal Base

Ingredients

⅓ cup old-fashioned rolled oats

1 tablespoon oat flour

1 teaspoon chia seeds

Sea salt

⅔ cup boiling water

1. In an 8-ounce glass jar or container with a lid, combine the oats, oat flour, chia seeds, and a pinch of salt. Give it a quick stir. Pour in the boiling water, stir well, cover with a lid, and let sit for 5 minutes.

Banana Bread

Ingredients

½ ripe banana, mashed

2 tablespoons chopped raw walnuts, divided

½ teaspoon cinnamon

Ground nutmeg

1½ teaspoons pure maple syrup

1. Prepare the Instant Oatmeal Base.

2. Stir in the mashed banana, 1 tablespoon of the walnuts, cinnamon, and a pinch of nutmeg. Sprinkle with the remaining 1 tablespoon walnuts and drizzle with the maple syrup.

Chocolate Peanut Butter

Ingredients

½ ripe banana, mashed

1 tablespoon cacao powder

1½ teaspoons pure maple syrup

3 teaspoons natural peanut butter, divided

1 tablespoon chopped roasted peanuts

1. Prepare the Instant Oatmeal Base.

2. Stir in the mashed banana, cacao powder, maple syrup, and 1½ teaspoons of the peanut butter. Top with the remaining 1½ teaspoons peanut butter and sprinkle the chopped peanuts on top.

recipe continues

Apple Cinnamon

Ingredients

2 tablespoons unsweetened
　applesauce

1½ teaspoons pure maple syrup

½ teaspoon cinnamon

¼ apple (Pink Lady or Fuji),
　sliced or chopped

1. Prepare the Instant Oatmeal Base.

2. Stir in the applesauce, maple syrup, and cinnamon. Top with the apple.

Strawberry Cheesecake

Ingredients

2 tablespoons plain full-fat Greek
　yogurt or coconut yogurt

3 teaspoons pure maple syrup,
　divided

1 teaspoon lemon zest

1 tablespoon fresh lemon juice

½ teaspoon pure vanilla extract

2 fresh strawberries, chopped

1. Prepare the Instant Oatmeal Base.

2. Stir in the yogurt, 1½ teaspoons of the maple syrup, lemon zest, lemon juice, and vanilla. Top with the chopped strawberries and drizzle with the remaining 1½ teaspoons maple syrup.

Orange Blueberry Almond

Ingredients

2 tablespoons plain full-fat Greek
　yogurt or coconut yogurt

2 tablespoons sliced blanched
　almonds, divided

3 teaspoons pure maple syrup,
　divided

1 teaspoon orange zest

1 tablespoon fresh orange juice

½ teaspoon pure almond extract

¼ cup fresh blueberries

1. Prepare the Instant Oatmeal Base.

2. Stir in the yogurt, 1 tablespoon of the sliced almonds, 1½ teaspoons of the maple syrup, orange zest, orange juice, and almond extract. Top with the remaining 1 tablespoon almonds, blueberries, and the remaining 1½ teaspoons maple syrup.

VARIATION　Swap out the old-fashioned oats for quick-cooking oats for a creamier texture.

Golden Chai Turmeric Oatmeal

Serves 2 • Prep Time 5 minutes • Cook Time 20 to 25 minutes

Prep Ahead

Vanilla Roasted Almond Butter
   (page 228)

Ingredients

2 cups water

Sea salt

1 teaspoon ghee

1 cup old-fashioned rolled oats

½ teaspoon ground turmeric

½ teaspoon cinnamon

¼ teaspoon ground ginger
   (or 1 teaspoon grated peeled
   fresh ginger)

Pepper

½ ripe banana

½ cup unsweetened coconut milk
   (from the carton), divided

¼ teaspoon pure vanilla extract

Toppings

½ cup fresh raspberries

2 tablespoons Vanilla Roasted
   Almond Butter

2 teaspoons pure liquid honey

2 tablespoons sliced blanched
   almonds

Turn your morning oatmeal into a vibrant golden dish with warming spices like turmeric, ginger, and cinnamon. Turmeric has many healing properties, so I try to sneak it into as many dishes as I can; its mild aromatic flavour pairs well with many foods. Creamy coconut milk, honey, and fresh berries on top make this a hearty and sweet breakfast-in-a-bowl. I love enjoying this on cool mornings with a mug of herbal coffee as I put together my to-do list for the day.

1. In a medium saucepan, bring the water to a boil with a pinch of salt over high heat.

2. In a large skillet, melt the ghee over medium-high heat. Stir in the oats and lightly toast for 2 to 3 minutes, until lightly golden, stirring often. Add the turmeric, cinnamon, ginger, and a pinch of pepper and toast, for 30 to 45 seconds, until fragrant.

3. Stir the oat mixture into the boiling water. Reduce the heat to a simmer, cover, and cook for 10 minutes, stirring occasionally.

4. Mash the banana into the oatmeal. Add ¼ cup of the coconut milk and the vanilla. Stir well, cover, and cook for 5 minutes. Remove from the heat and allow to sit for 5 minutes.

5. Divide the oatmeal between 2 bowls. Top with fresh raspberries, Vanilla Roasted Almond Butter, and the remaining ¼ cup coconut milk. Drizzle with honey, sprinkle with sliced almonds, and serve warm.

🌰 **HEALTHNUT TIP** Black pepper in oatmeal? No, this is not a mistake. Black pepper helps your body absorb the nutrients from the turmeric—science!

Meal prep
- Green smoothies
- kale salad
- sweet potatoes roas
- french dressing

To Do List:
☑ film meal prep video
☐ Edit thumbnails
☐ grocery shop
☐ Meeting @1:30pm
☐ Call Mr. Matt back
☐ clean out fridge

be heard

Salted Caramel Stovetop Granola

Makes 4 cups • **Prep Time 15 minutes** • **Cook Time 10 minutes** • **Chill Time 10 to 15 minutes**

Prep Ahead

Salted Caramel Butter (page 233)

Ingredients

1 teaspoon coconut oil

2 cups old-fashioned rolled oats

½ cup raw almonds, roughly
    chopped

¼ cup raw sunflower seeds

¼ cup raw pumpkin seeds

½ teaspoon cinnamon

½ cup Salted Caramel Butter,
    warmed

There is nothing like warm homemade granola straight out of the oven. But did you know you can make granola, with the same toasted flavour, right on your stovetop? Yup! No oven necessary! Plus, it cooks in a third of the time and you're left with clustered, slightly chewy granola that no one will guess took you only 10 minutes to cook. I'm all about healthy hacks to make life easier, and this one sure ticks the boxes. Serve on smoothie bowls or yogurt, or as a breakfast cereal with nut milk and fruit.

1. Line a baking sheet with parchment paper. Melt the coconut oil in a large skillet over medium-high heat. Add the oats, almonds, sunflower seeds, pumpkin seeds, and cinnamon. Gently toss until well combined. Cook for 8 to 10 minutes, stirring constantly, until the oats and nuts are toasty golden and fragrant. Remove from the heat.

2. Drizzle the warm Salted Caramel Butter over the granola and stir until evenly coated. Spread the granola onto the prepared baking sheet and then, using a spatula, press the granola firmly together and flatten it evenly. Refrigerate for 10 to 15 minutes to cool and set.

3. Break into chunks or crumble. Store in an airtight container at room temperature for up to 1 month or in the freezer for up to 2 months.

🌰 **HEALTHNUT TIP** Use brown rice syrup as a sweetener in recipes with oats or puffed grains to create a sweet, crispy but chewy texture when set. Think chewy granola bars and rice crispy squares.

Strawberry Banana Chia Breakfast Jar

Serves 3 • Prep Time 5 minutes • Chill Time 30 minutes

Prep Ahead (optional)

Salted Caramel Stovetop Granola
(page 41)

Chia Pudding

⅓ cup chia seeds

1⅓ cups canned full-fat coconut
milk

1 tablespoon pure maple syrup

1 teaspoon pure vanilla extract

Smoothie Layer

1 frozen ripe medium banana,
roughly chopped

½ cup frozen strawberries

⅓ to ½ cup unsweetened almond
milk or coconut milk (from the
carton)

Toppings

1 small ripe banana, sliced

4 fresh strawberries, cut in half

¼ cup Salted Caramel Stovetop
Granola (optional)

To chia or to smoothie? For days when you just can't decide on what to have for breakfast, just have both! This layered parfait has the fun texture of chia pudding with the smooth consistency and tart flavour of a strawberry banana smoothie. Fruit on the bottom and pudding on the top—just like your favourite yogurt cups, but with way more fun and fibre! This is a breakfast you'll be coming back to again and again.

1. Make the Chia Pudding In a medium bowl, whisk together the chia seeds, coconut milk, maple syrup, and vanilla. Cover and refrigerate for 30 minutes to help thicken (or up to 1 hour or overnight), stirring with a whisk after 15 minutes to prevent the chia seeds from clumping together.

2. Make the Smoothie Layer In a high-speed blender, combine the banana, strawberries, and ⅓ cup of the almond milk. Blend on high speed for 1 minute, or until smooth, adding more milk if needed to help blend. You should have a thick smoothie consistency.

3. Assemble the Chia Breakfast Jar Divide the chia pudding among 2-cup glass jars, then pour the smoothie over the pudding. Top with sliced banana, sliced strawberries, and Salted Caramel Stovetop Granola (if using) and enjoy!

VARIATION Have fun and use whatever frozen fruit you have in the freezer. Try flavour combinations like mango lime, raspberry lemon, or mixed berry.

HEALTHNUT TIP If you'd like a lighter version, you can replace the canned coconut milk with carton coconut milk—but the pudding will not be as creamy and will take longer to thicken up. You can prep the chia pudding ahead so it's ready to go in the morning. Store the chia pudding in an airtight container in the fridge for up to 5 days.

Good Morning Breakfast Salad

Serves 2 • **Prep Time 10 minutes**

. . . .

Prep Ahead

Jammy Eggs (page 218)

Salted Caramel Stovetop Granola
(page 41)

**Orange Maple Cinnamon
Dressing**

Juice of ½ orange

¼ cup extra-virgin olive oil

1 tablespoon pure maple syrup

¼ teaspoon apple cider vinegar

¼ teaspoon cinnamon

Sea salt

Breakfast Salad

3 cups loosely packed spring
mix greens

1 cup fresh strawberries, quartered

5 or 6 orange segments, cut in half

½ large ripe avocado, pitted,
peeled, and sliced

2 Jammy Eggs, sliced

¼ cup Salted Caramel Stovetop
Granola

Sea salt and pepper

Salad for breakfast? You bet! This bowl of mixed greens is full of fresh fruits like strawberries, oranges, and avocados (yes, they're a fruit) and topped with my Jammy Eggs (page 218) and a sprinkle of Salted Caramel Stovetop Granola (page 41) for an unexpected crunch. Not to mention that the dressing for this salad—made with cinnamon, maple syrup, and orange juice—is the most delicious thing ever and tastes like Sunday brunch without the hollandaise or mimosas.

1. **Make the Orange Maple Cinnamon Dressing** In a small glass jar, combine the orange juice, olive oil, maple syrup, cider vinegar, cinnamon, and a pinch of salt. Cover and shake well.

2. **Make the Breakfast Salad** In a large salad bowl, combine the greens, strawberries, and oranges. Toss with desired amount of dressing. (Store any remaining dressing in the jar in the fridge for up to 4 days.)

3. Divide the salad between 2 bowls. Top with avocado, Jammy Eggs, and Salted Caramel Stovetop Granola. Season the eggs with salt and pepper and enjoy.

VARIATION Swap the Salted Caramel Stovetop Granola (page 41) for raw walnuts and the strawberries for raspberries.

🌰 **HEALTHNUT TIP** Make the dressing and eggs up to 2 days ahead. Prepare your salad ingredients throughout the week for a speedy prep on busy mornings.

Sunday Brunch Bowl

Serves 2 • Prep Time 10 minutes • Cook Time 30 to 35 minutes

Prep Ahead

Fluffy Scrambled Eggs (page 217)

Crispy Oven Bacon (page 222)

Ingredients

10 mini potatoes (½ pound/225 g),
    quartered

1 tablespoon fresh lemon juice

4 teaspoons ghee or extra-virgin
    olive oil, divided

1 teaspoon fresh thyme leaves

Sweet paprika

Sea salt and pepper

1 cup button mushrooms
    (about 3 ounces/85 g)

10 cherry tomatoes
    (about 3 ounces/85 g)

1 clove garlic, minced

4 cups loosely packed fresh baby
    spinach

1 batch Fluffy Scrambled Eggs

6 strips Crispy Oven Bacon

What's better than breakfast? Brunch, of course! This scrumptious brunch bowl is just the thing you need to get you out of bed and fuelled for the weekend. Sautéed veggies, crispy spuds, bacon, and soft, pillowy scrambled eggs all come together in one convenient bowl. Cheers to sleeping in and drinking champagne with orange juice before noon!

1. Preheat the oven to 400°F. Line a baking sheet with parchment paper.

2. In a medium bowl, combine the potatoes, lemon juice, 2 teaspoons of the ghee, thyme, and a pinch each of paprika, salt, and pepper. Toss to coat well. Spread the potatoes on the prepared baking sheet and bake for 10 minutes. Toss and bake for another 10 to 12 minutes, until fork-tender on the inside and crispy on the outside.

3. Meanwhile, in a large skillet, melt the remaining 2 teaspoons ghee over medium-high heat. Add the mushrooms and tomatoes and sauté for 8 minutes. Add the garlic and sauté for another minute. Add the spinach and a pinch each of salt and pepper, stir well, cover, and cook for 3 minutes.

4. Divide the potatoes and veggies between 2 bowls. Top with Fluffy Scrambled Eggs and arrange the Crispy Oven Bacon on the side. Season with salt and pepper and serve.

Everyday Gluten-Free Fluffy Pancakes

Makes 8 pancakes • Prep Time 5 minutes • Cook Time 10 minutes

Ingredients

1 ripe medium banana, mashed

2 eggs

½ cup unsweetened almond milk
   or coconut milk (from the carton)

2 tablespoons coconut oil, melted

1 teaspoon pure vanilla extract

1 cup brown rice flour

2 teaspoons baking powder

½ teaspoon cinnamon

Sea salt

Coconut oil or organic unsalted
   butter, for cooking

Toppings

Natural peanut butter

Fresh raspberries

Raw sunflower seeds

Pure maple syrup

These are the fluffiest pancakes you'll ever make, with simple, on-hand ingredients like eggs, flour, and cinnamon. Every family needs a go-to pancake recipe, and this is it. Fluffy, tender, and naturally sweetened with mashed banana, these are everything you want in a stack of Sunday morning pancakes piled high on your plate. Double or triple the recipe because, I promise you, these will go quick!

1. Preheat the oven to 200°F. Line a baking sheet with parchment paper.

2. In a medium bowl, mash the banana with a fork until it's smooth but still has some visible pieces of fruit. Whisk in the eggs, almond milk, melted coconut oil, and vanilla to combine.

3. Sift in the brown rice flour, baking powder, cinnamon, and a pinch of salt. Mix with the whisk or a rubber spatula until the batter is smooth with some lumps. If the batter is too wet, add more flour, a heaping teaspoon at a time. If the batter is too dry, add a splash of milk. You want a thick cake-like batter so the pancakes are fluffy and don't spread out too much on the pan.

4. Heat a large non-stick skillet over medium-low heat with 1 teaspoon of coconut oil. Add about ¼ cup of batter for each pancake. Cover and cook until the bottom is golden brown, 2 to 3 minutes. You'll know they are ready to flip once the edges start to round and firm up and bubbles start to form on top. Flip and continue to cook until golden brown on the bottom, another 2 to 3 minutes. Transfer to the baking sheet and keep warm in the oven while you cook the remaining pancakes.

5. Serve the pancakes warm, drizzled with maple syrup and topped with natural peanut butter, fresh raspberries, and sunflower seeds, if you really want to go all out!

VARIATION Fold ½ cup of fresh or frozen blueberries or ¼ cup chocolate chips into the batter for a fun burst of flavour in every bite.

HEALTHNUT TIP Do not overmix the batter! One of the biggest mistakes with pancakes is overmixing. If you overmix you'll get rid of all the air bubbles and flour lumps, making your pancakes fall flat instead of staying fluffy while cooking. Store any leftover cooled pancakes in a resealable freezer bag in the freezer for up to 1 month. When ready to eat, pop them into the toaster until heated through.

Green Smoothie Pancakes

Serves 2 to 4 (makes 7 to 8 pancakes) • Prep Time 5 minutes • Cook Time 15 minutes

Ingredients

1 ripe medium banana, roughly
    chopped
2 eggs
½ cup unsweetened almond milk or
    coconut milk (from the carton)
1 tablespoon natural almond butter
1 teaspoon pure vanilla extract
1 cup loosely packed fresh baby
    spinach
1 cup oat flour
1 tablespoon ground flaxseed
2 teaspoons baking powder
¼ teaspoon cinnamon
Sea salt (omit if using salted almond
    butter)
1 tablespoon ghee or organic
    unsalted butter, for cooking

Toppings (optional)

Blueberries
Sliced banana
Natural almond butter
Pure maple syrup

On days when I can't decide whether to have pancakes or a smoothie for breakfast, why not just have both! In this recipe I've taken all the fun ingredients in a morning smoothie and packed them into delicious, fluffy, vibrant green pancakes even Popeye would approve of. The best part? All the ingredients are combined in a blender so you can have pancakes in minutes.

1. Preheat the oven to 200°F. Line a baking sheet with parchment paper.

2. In a high-speed blender, combine the banana, eggs, almond milk, almond butter, vanilla, and spinach. Process for 15 to 20 seconds, until smooth.

3. Add the oat flour, flaxseed, baking powder, cinnamon, and a pinch of salt, if using. Pulse for about 5 seconds. Try not to overblend the batter. You want some lumps and air bubbles, otherwise your pancakes will not be as fluffy. Let the batter sit for 5 minutes.

4. Heat a large non-stick skillet over medium heat. Lightly grease with ghee, wiping with paper towel. Pour about ¼ cup batter into the skillet for each pancake. Cover and cook for 3 to 4 minutes, until soft bubbles form on top and the edges start to firm up. Flip and cook for another 1 to 2 minutes until lightly golden. Transfer to the prepared baking sheet and keep warm in the oven while you cook the remaining pancakes. Repeat until all the batter is used, greasing the pan in between batches.

5. To serve, top the warm pancakes with your choice of toppings and a drizzle of maple syrup. Store any leftovers in an airtight container in the fridge for up to 4 days. Reheat in the toaster and enjoy!

🌰 **HEALTHNUT TIP** If you only have whole flaxseeds and rolled oats on hand, simply grind them separately in your blender to make ground flaxseed and oat flour in seconds. Just be sure to do this before starting the recipe so your blender is dry.

Dutch Baby Pancake

Serves 4 to 6 • Prep Time 5 minutes • Bake Time 17 minutes

Prep Ahead (optional)
Coconut Whip (page 231)

Ingredients
3 eggs
¾ cup unsweetened almond milk or
   coconut milk (from the carton)
2 tablespoons pure liquid honey
1 teaspoon pure vanilla extract
¾ cup brown rice flour
Sea salt
1 tablespoon ghee or organic
   unsalted butter

Toppings
1 cup frozen mixed berries
¼ cup plain full-fat Greek yogurt,
   coconut yogurt, or Coconut Whip
Wedge of lemon
1 to 2 tablespoons pure maple syrup
Fresh mint, for garnish (optional)

Simple yet gourmet, this pancake dish is sure to impress your family and friends. Think crepe meets pancake with an eggy custard flavour. Not only does it take 5 minutes to mix up, but the way the pancake puffs up in the oven makes for a beautiful work of food art that will make you want to turn the oven light on and take a peek. This is the perfect dish to celebrate the weekend with.

1. Place a large cast-iron skillet in the oven and preheat the oven to 425°F.

2. In a medium bowl, whisk together the eggs, almond milk, honey, and vanilla. Add the brown rice flour and a pinch of salt; stir until well combined.

3. Carefully remove the hot skillet from the oven and add the ghee. Swirl the pan until the ghee is melted and the skillet is well coated. Pour the batter into the skillet. Bake for 17 minutes, or until the pancake is puffed and lightly browned on top.

4. Meanwhile, in a small saucepan, heat the frozen berries over medium-low heat, covered and stirring occasionally, until warm and syrupy, 6 to 8 minutes.

5. Remove the pancake from the oven and let it sit for 2 to 3 minutes. Top with the warm berries, yogurt, a squeeze of lemon juice, and a drizzle of maple syrup. Garnish with fresh mint, if using, and serve immediately, right from the skillet.

🌰 **HEALTHNUT TIP** For a taller Dutch baby pancake, use eggs and milk that are at room temperature. To save time in the morning, make the batter the night before and refrigerate it overnight.

Jalapeño Pumpkin Waffles

Makes 6 waffles • Prep Time 5 minutes • Cook Time 20 minutes

Ingredients

1 cup canned pure pumpkin purée

1½ cups unsweetened almond milk
  or coconut milk (from the carton)

2 eggs

2 tablespoons pure maple syrup

2 tablespoons coconut oil, melted

1½ cups brown rice flour

1 tablespoon nutritional yeast

2 teaspoons baking powder

½ teaspoon sea salt

¼ teaspoon black pepper

¼ teaspoon smoked paprika

¼ teaspoon ground nutmeg

1 jalapeño pepper, seeded and
  finely chopped

Pure maple syrup, for serving

Team pancakes or waffles? I always thought I was a pancake girl until I discovered the wonders of a waffle iron. You can pretty much waffle-ize anything your heart desires—including pumpkin and jalapeño peppers! These waffles are savoury with a hint of spice. They pair perfectly with a simple drizzle of maple syrup or, for something more substantial, my Baked Crispy Quinoa Chicken Fingers (page 180). Think of them as the perfect base for all your delicious toppings.

1. Preheat a waffle iron on high heat. Preheat the oven to 200°F and set a rack in a baking sheet.

2. In a large bowl, combine the pumpkin purée, almond milk, eggs, maple syrup, and coconut oil. Whisk until blended.

3. Add the brown rice flour, nutritional yeast, baking powder, salt, black pepper, paprika, and nutmeg. Whisk until well combined. Fold in the jalapeño. The batter should be thick and smooth.

4. Brush both sides of the waffle iron with coconut oil. Pour about ½ cup of the batter into the waffle iron and cook for 3 to 4 minutes, until golden with crispy edges. Remove the waffle by gently loosening an edge with a heatproof rubber spatula or tongs, transfer to the baking sheet, and keep warm in the oven. Repeat until all the batter is used. Enjoy with maple syrup and your favourite toppings.

HEALTHNUT TIP When buying pumpkin purée, be careful not to pick up pumpkin pie filling—they're easily mixed up and taste very different! Store any leftover cooled waffles in a resealable freezer bag in the freezer for up to 1 month. For a quick breakfast in minutes, pop them into the toaster until heated through.

Eggs Benny on a Crepe

Serves 2 • Prep Time 5 minutes • Cook Time 10 to 12 minutes

Prep Ahead
Easy Blender Crepes (page 220)

Filling
1 tablespoon extra-virgin olive oil
1 clove garlic, minced
8 spears of asparagus, trimmed
2 cups lightly packed fresh baby
   spinach
1 tablespoon water
Sea salt and pepper
4 slices smoked salmon
   (about 4 ounces/115 g)

Turmeric Poached Eggs
1 tablespoon apple cider vinegar
¼ teaspoon ground turmeric
Sea salt and pepper
2 eggs
2 Easy Blender Crepes

My go-to indulgent brunch pick is good old-fashioned eggs Benedict. But honestly, who needs that heavy hollandaise sauce full of mostly butter when you have perfectly poached eggs? The runny yolk is a much healthier option and will give your non-traditional eggs Benedict that perfect sauciness it needs when you break into it.

1. Make the Filling In a medium non-stick skillet, heat the olive oil over medium heat. Add the garlic and cook, stirring, for 1 minute or until fragrant. Add the asparagus and cook, stirring, for about 2 minutes. Add the spinach on top of the asparagus with the water, and a pinch each of salt and pepper, cover, and cook for 2 to 3 minutes, until the spinach is wilted. Remove from the heat.

2. Make the Turmeric Poached Eggs Pour a couple of inches of water into a medium saucepan and bring to a simmer over medium heat. Whisk in the cider vinegar, turmeric, and a pinch of salt. Crack 1 egg into a small bowl. Using a butter knife, stir the water to create a swirl and then slowly slide the egg into the water. Wait 30 to 60 seconds to allow the egg white to cook slightly and stay together and then gently swirl the water next to the first egg before adding the second egg. Cook each egg for about 3 minutes for a runny yolk. Gently remove the poached egg using a slotted spoon, tap off excess water, transfer to a plate, and season with a pinch each of salt and pepper.

3. To assemble, place a crepe flat on each plate and arrange half of the asparagus and spinach mixture down one side of each crepe. Top each with 2 slices of smoked salmon. Fold the crepes in half to cover the filling. Place a Turmeric Poached Egg on top and dig in!

VARIATION Swap out the smoked salmon for Crispy Oven Bacon (page 222) or crumbled soft goat cheese.

🥜 HEALTHNUT TIP Properly poached eggs can take some practice, so if you've never done it before, just cook one at a time until you're a poaching master.

AB & J Coconut Yogurt Crepes

Serves 4 • **Prep Time 5 minutes**

Prep Ahead

Easy Blender Crepes (page 220)

Vanilla Roasted Almond Butter
    (page 228)

Sunshine Berry Chia Jam (page 60)

Ingredients

1 batch Easy Blender Crepes

¼ cup Vanilla Roasted Almond Butter

¼ cup Sunshine Berry Chia Jam

¼ cup plain full-fat Greek yogurt or
    coconut yogurt

2 ripe medium bananas, halved
    lengthwise

Toppings (optional)

Pure maple syrup

Cinnamon

This is one of those recipes that created itself on a morning when I was in a rush and a quick breakfast was desperately needed. Simple crepes with simple fillings that'll take you back to your peanut-butter-and-jelly childhood days. This crepe is perfect as a throw-together breakfast because you can just roll it up and eat it with one hand as you're heading out the door. Even better, enjoy it on a plate with a fork and knife while sipping your favourite morning tea and listening to a good podcast.

1. Place a crepe flat on a plate and spread 1 tablespoon each of Vanilla Roasted Almond Butter, Sunshine Berry Chai Jam, and yogurt over the centre, leaving about a ½-inch border around the edges. Place a banana half on the bottom edge of the crepe and roll it up. Drizzle with maple syrup and sprinkle with cinnamon, if using. Repeat to fill the remaining crepes and enjoy!

🌰 **HEALTHNUT TIP** These roll-ups are also great as a mid-afternoon or post-workout protein power snack.

Apple Maple Breakfast Sausage Patties

Makes 12 to 14 patties • **Prep Time 5 minutes** • **Cook Time 6 to 8 minutes**

Ingredients

1 pound (450 g) lean ground pork

1 pound (450 g) lean ground turkey
 or chicken

2 cloves garlic, minced

½ cup unsweetened applesauce

3 tablespoons pure maple syrup

2 teaspoons sea salt

2 teaspoons fresh thyme leaves
 (or 1 teaspoon dried thyme)

1 teaspoon fennel seeds

½ teaspoon ground sage

½ teaspoon pepper

¼ teaspoon ground nutmeg

¼ teaspoon sweet paprika

1 teaspoon avocado oil

Store-bought processed meats usually contain a whole whack of not-so-great ingredients like sulphates, excess sodium, and things I can't even pronounce. Once I discovered how simple it was to make my own sausage patties, I haven't looked back. Sweetened with natural ingredients like applesauce and pure maple syrup, and with complementing herbs and spices like fennel, sage, thyme, and nutmeg, this sausage has the perfect savoury-sweet combo. Serve hot as a side, in a breakfast sandwich, or with Fluffy Scrambled Eggs (page 217) and Maple "Baked" Beans (page 183).

1. In a large bowl, combine the pork, turkey, garlic, applesauce, maple syrup, salt, thyme, fennel, sage, pepper, nutmeg, and paprika. Using your hands, mix well.

2. Scoop out ¼ cup of the mixture at a time and shape into 12 to 14 patties about ½ inch thick. Set aside on a large plate.

3. Heat the avocado oil in a large non-stick skillet or griddle over medium-high heat. Fry the patties, in batches if necessary, for 3 to 4 minutes on each side, until golden brown and cooked through. Store any leftovers in an airtight container in the fridge for up to 3 days.

HEALTHNUT TIP You can freeze these patties raw or cooked. Layer them individually between pieces of parchment paper and store in a resealable freezer bag in the freezer for up to 1 month. When ready to use, simply transfer the bag to the fridge the night before to thaw. Cook or reheat in an oiled skillet.

Sunshine Berry Chia Jam

Makes ¾ cup • **Prep Time 5 minutes** • **Chill Time 1 hour**

Ingredients

1 cup fresh raspberries or
   blackberries

2 tablespoons ground chia seeds

1 tablespoon fresh orange juice

1 tablespoon fresh lemon juice

1 to 2 tablespoons pure maple syrup

¼ teaspoon citric acid or sea salt

Strawberry jam used to be one of my favourite things when I was growing up. Little did I know how much processed sugar was in one little jar! Did you know that for something to be called jam, it must have a sugar content of at least 60 percent? Nowadays I enjoy making this naturally sweetened version with fresh berries, citrus, pure maple syrup, and chia seeds (a.k.a. mini dinosaur eggs) to thicken everything up and add a great boost of fibre to my morning toast. So although I may not technically be allowed to call this recipe "jam," it's a perfect complement to my Everyday Nut and Seed Loaf (page 91).

1. In a small food processor, combine the raspberries, chia seeds, orange juice, lemon juice, maple syrup (start with 1 tablespoon and adjust sweetness to your liking), and citric acid. Process for 10 seconds.

2. Scrape the jam into a small glass jar with a lid and let sit in the fridge to thicken, about 1 hour. (You can also enjoy the jam right away but it won't have a thick, jammy texture just yet.) Store in the fridge for up to 2 weeks if made with citric acid or up to 1 week if with made with salt.

VARIATION Use half raspberries and half blackberries for a mixed-berry jam.

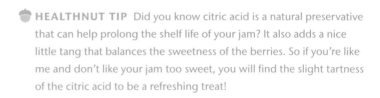 **HEALTHNUT TIP** Did you know citric acid is a natural preservative that can help prolong the shelf life of your jam? It also adds a nice little tang that balances the sweetness of the berries. So if you're like me and don't like your jam too sweet, you will find the slight tartness of the citric acid to be a refreshing treat!

Sweet Potato Hash Browns

Makes 6 patties • **Prep Time 5 minutes** • **Cook Time 20 minutes**

Prep Ahead
Cumin Yogurt Dip (see page 172)

Ingredients
1 egg
2 small sweet potatoes, peeled
   and shredded (about 2½ cups)
1 shallot, shredded
1 tablespoon fresh lemon juice
½ cup chickpea flour
1 teaspoon garlic powder
½ teaspoon baking powder
½ teaspoon sea salt
¼ teaspoon pepper
¼ teaspoon ground cumin
¼ teaspoon smoked paprika
1 to 2 tablespoons avocado oil
Chopped green onion (white and
   light green parts only), for garnish
1 batch Cumin Yogurt Dip,
   for serving

These sweet potato hash browns—or as I like to call them, "potato pancakes"—are just the right amount of savoury and sweet. Crispy on the outside and soft and tender on the inside, they are delicious topped with some Crispy Oven Bacon (page 222) or a Sunny-Side-Up Egg (page 218)—or with both! You decide!

1. In a large bowl, lightly beat the egg. Stir in the sweet potato, shallot, and lemon juice. Add the chickpea flour, garlic powder, baking powder, salt, pepper, cumin, and paprika and mix well.

2. In a large non-stick skillet, heat 1 to 2 tablespoons of avocado oil over medium-high heat. Scoop ¼ cup of sweet potato batter per hash brown, shape into patties, and place in the skillet. Cover and cook for 4 to 6 minutes on each side, until golden brown and the edges are crispy. Repeat until all the sweet potato mixture is cooked.

3. Serve warm, garnished with green onions. Serve the Cumin Yogurt Dip on the side.

🌰 **HEALTHNUT TIP** For the best shredded sweet potato, I like using the grater attachment on my food processor. It's not only quicker with better shreds, but your fingers will stay safe!

Naked Samosa Hash

Serves 4 • **Prep Time 5 minutes** • **Cook Time 25 to 30 minutes**

Ingredients

1½ teaspoons garam masala

½ teaspoon cumin seeds

½ teaspoon ground cumin

½ teaspoon red chili flakes

¼ teaspoon ground turmeric

⅛ teaspoon ground cardamom

2 tablespoons avocado oil

1 shallot, chopped

½-inch piece fresh ginger,
   peeled and grated

3 medium Yukon Gold potatoes,
   peeled and cut into ½-inch cubes
   (about 4 cups)

1 teaspoon sea salt

¼ teaspoon black pepper

½ cup low-sodium vegetable stock

1 cup fresh or frozen peas

2 tablespoons fresh lemon juice

Garnishes

Sweet paprika

1 to 2 tablespoons chopped fresh
   cilantro

I love tasting flavours from other cultures, so when I discovered the wonders of the samosa I was instantly inspired. This "naked" version of the traditional triangle-shaped Indian pastry is a flavourful addition to any brunch. Let's be honest, the good stuff is all in the middle anyway, so I made a recipe of just that—the filling and nothing else. Now if I could just stop mixing up the words "samosa" and "mimosa," I would be all set! Enjoy these on their own as a main or on the side with my Crispy Oven Bacon (page 222).

1. In a small bowl, stir together the garam masala, cumin seeds, ground cumin, chili flakes, turmeric, and cardamom.

2. Heat the avocado oil in a large skillet over medium-high heat. Add the spice mixture and stir for 1 minute to release the flavours of the spices, being careful not to burn the spices. Reduce the heat to medium, add the shallot and grated ginger, and cook, stirring, for 2 minutes.

3. Add the potatoes and season with salt and black pepper. Stir until the potatoes are evenly coated with the spices, then fry until the edges are crisp, about 12 minutes. Stir in the vegetable stock, cover, and cook for 8 to 10 minutes, until the potatoes are fork-tender, stirring occasionally.

4. Stir in the peas and lemon juice and cook for 2 minutes. Transfer to a serving plate and garnish with a sprinkle of paprika and cilantro before serving.

HEALTHNUT TIP This hash is even better as leftovers for lunch or dinner the next day. Top with a fried egg and sliced avocado for a complete meal. For this reason alone, you'll want to make extra!

Skillet Shakshuka

Serves 4 to 6 • Prep Time 8 to 10 minutes • Cook Time 20 to 25 minutes

Ingredients

2 tablespoons extra-virgin olive oil

1 medium yellow onion, finely chopped

4 cloves garlic, minced

½ cayenne chili pepper, seeded and finely chopped

4 vine-ripened tomatoes, diced

1 medium sweet red pepper, diced

1 teaspoon sweet paprika

½ teaspoon ground cumin

½ teaspoon ground coriander

½ teaspoon sea salt

¼ teaspoon black pepper

1 can (19 ounces/540 mL) diced tomatoes

1 tablespoon tomato paste

1½ teaspoons pure maple syrup

4 to 6 eggs

2 tablespoons chopped fresh cilantro, for garnish

¼ cup whole Kalamata olives, pitted, for garnish

Toasted sourdough bread or Everyday Nut and Seed Loaf (page 91), for serving

My take on the Middle Eastern traditional dish that's both spicy and hearty with a range of deep flavours like tomato, cumin, coriander, and paprika. This is one of those dishes that looks complicated to make but in reality is super simple to put together. A rich red pepper tomato sauce cooked down to perfection in less than 30 minutes. Bonus: this recipe only requires one pot. Great flavours, fewer dishes—win-win!

1. Heat the olive oil in a large cast-iron skillet over medium heat.

2. Add the onion, garlic, and chili pepper and cook for 2 minutes, stirring occasionally.

3. Increase the heat to medium-high and add the vine-ripened tomatoes, red pepper, paprika, cumin, coriander, salt, and black pepper. Stir well. Cook for 5 minutes, mashing the tomatoes with a wooden spoon.

4. Stir in the canned diced tomatoes, tomato paste, and maple syrup. Reduce the heat and simmer for 10 minutes, stirring occasionally.

5. With the back of a spoon, make 4 to 6 small indentations in the tomato mixture, making sure they are evenly spaced. Gently crack an egg directly into each well and spoon a bit of sauce over the egg whites, leaving the yolk exposed. Reduce the heat to low, cover, and cook until the egg whites are fully cooked but the yolk is still runny.

6. Garnish with cilantro and olives and enjoy nice and hot with a slice of your favourite toast for dipping.

🌰 **HEALTHNUT TIP** If you can't find fresh cayenne chili peppers, use ¼ teaspoon dried red chili flakes. This tomato and pepper sauce is also great as a pasta sauce for spaghetti and meatballs night.

Curry Mushroom Spinach Omelette

Serves 1 or 2 • **Prep Time 5 minutes** • **Cook Time 10 minutes**

Ingredients

4 eggs

2 tablespoons unsweetened almond milk or coconut milk

¼ teaspoon curry powder

Sea salt and pepper

2 teaspoons ghee or organic unsalted butter, divided

½ shallot, thinly sliced

1 clove garlic, minced

1 cup sliced mushrooms (I like shimeji)

3 cups lightly packed fresh baby spinach

Omelettes for me are great for any meal of the day. I love that you can add almost any veggie or seasoning you want and still serve up a deliciously fluffy egg dish. This recipe was inspired by my best friend since grade six, Yvonne. During one of our weekly Monday night workouts, she offered to whip up dinner (a.k.a. breakfast), and she spontaneously decided to add curry powder. I instantly fell in love! The curry is subtle enough to keep this omelette "breakfast friendly," but it adds a ton of flavour and depth to the eggs. Not to mention, it's a great post-workout meal!

1. In a medium bowl, whisk together the eggs, almond milk, curry powder, and a pinch each of salt and pepper. Set aside.

2. In a medium non-stick skillet, melt 1 teaspoon of the ghee over medium heat. Add the shallot and garlic and cook, stirring, for 1 minute. Add the mushrooms and cook for 2 minutes, stirring often. Add the spinach and 1 tablespoon of water, stir, cover, and cook for 1 to 2 minutes until slightly wilted. Transfer the veggies to a small bowl.

3. Wipe the skillet clean and melt the remaining 1 teaspoon ghee over medium-low heat. Pour in the egg mixture, cover, and cook for 2 to 4 minutes until the eggs are almost set. Spread the cooked veggies over one half of the omelette and fold the other side over the filling. Cover again and cook for another minute, and serve hot.

🌰 **HEALTHNUT TIP** The better the egg, the better the omelette! When possible, choose free-run and, even better, organic eggs. I promise you'll see and taste the difference.

BLT Fried Egg Breakfast Sammy

Serves 2 • Prep Time 10 minutes

Prep Ahead
Avocado Ranch Dip (page 229)

Crispy Oven Bacon (page 222)

Ingredients
4 slices sourdough or gluten-free
  bread

¼ cup Avocado Ranch Dip

6 small romaine lettuce leaves

1 heirloom tomato (cut into 6 slices)

6 strips Crispy Oven Bacon

2 Sunny-Side-Up Eggs (page 218)

There is nothing better than that feeling you get when you're trying to figure out what to have for lunch and then realize you have all the makings for a BLT. Am I right? Whoever thought of combining crispy bacon, juicy fresh tomato, and crunchy lettuce into one sandwich was seriously a genius! If you're as big a fan of the BLT as I am, then you're going to feel some serious love for this version, which has a fried egg and my Avocado Ranch Dip. My mouth is already watering just thinking about it!

1. Toast the bread. Spread 2 tablespoons of the Avocado Ranch Dip on each of 2 pieces of toast. Top each with 3 lettuce leaves, 3 slices of tomato, 3 slices of bacon, and 1 Sunny-Side-Up Egg, then top with the remaining pieces of toast.

HEALTHNUT TIP As a plant-based option, use tempeh bacon and tofu scramble to get a similar texture and flavour—a different incarnation, but just as cool!

Nourishing

SNACKS

and

DRINKS

Honey-Roasted Sriracha Cashews

Makes 2 cups • **Prep Time 5 minutes** • **Bake Time 16 to 18 minutes**

Ingredients

2 tablespoons pure liquid honey

1 tablespoon Sriracha

½ teaspoon ground ginger

½ teaspoon sea salt

¼ teaspoon pepper

2 cups unsalted whole raw cashews

1 teaspoon sesame seeds (I like
using a mix of black and white)

My boyfriend, Matt, insisted that I recreate this sweet and spicy snack after we bought a similar one from a bulk food store that listed hydrogenated oils and corn syrup among the ingredients. I quickly went to work and created my own healthier version that Matt now requests I make every week. This is a great power snack to bring with you on a hike, or toss in your salad for some extra-flavourful protein and crunch. Just don't have a bowl of them in front of you while watching Netflix—they won't make it to episode two!

1. Preheat the oven to 350°F. Line a baking sheet with parchment paper.

2. In a medium bowl, whisk together the honey, Sriracha, ginger, salt, and pepper. Add the cashews and stir and toss until well coated.

3. Using a rubber spatula, spread the nut mixture evenly on the prepared baking sheet. Sprinkle the sesame seeds evenly on top. Bake for 16 to 18 minutes, or until golden, tossing halfway through.

4. Let the cashews cool completely on the baking sheet before serving. Store in an airtight container at room temperature for up to 2 weeks.

VARIATION You can use any kind of nut. Try this with pecans or almonds, or go crazy and mix them up! Make a double batch for parties or as a Super Bowl snack.

No-Bake Coconut Almond Clusters

Makes 18 to 20 clusters • Prep Time 20 minutes • Cook Time 10 to 13 minutes • Chill Time 10 minutes

Ingredients

1 teaspoon ghee or coconut oil
1 cup sliced blanched almonds
1 cup unsweetened coconut flakes
¼ cup raw pumpkin seeds
¼ cup raw sunflower seeds
1 tablespoon chia seeds
½ teaspoon cinnamon
¼ teaspoon sea salt
3 tablespoons pure liquid honey

A sweet and salty cluster with my favourite nuts and seeds makes this a must-have crunchy treat to keep stocked in your snack cupboard. I love the crisp toasted coconut flakes and almond slices held together with some good-quality honey. Plus, there's no baking required! Snack with caution—these are dangerously addicting.

1. Line a baking sheet with parchment paper.

2. In a large skillet, melt the ghee over medium heat. Add the almonds, coconut flakes, pumpkin seeds, and sunflower seeds and toast for 5 to 7 minutes, until golden, stirring constantly to prevent burning.

3. Add the chia seeds, cinnamon, salt, and honey and stir until everything is evenly coated. Reduce the heat to low and cook for 2 minutes while stirring gently.

4. Remove from the heat and let cool slightly. Scoop 2 tablespoons of the mixture at a time and drop on the prepared baking sheet. You can gently push together each cluster with the back of a spoon to help them stick together better when set. Refrigerate for about 10 minutes, or until the clusters are cooled and set. Store in an airtight container at room temperature for up to 2 weeks.

VARIATION If you don't feel like scooping, spread the nut mixture evenly on the baking sheet, pressing it lightly with the back of a rubber spatula to keep the mixture together. Refrigerate for about 10 minutes, or until cool and set. Using your hands, break into desired size pieces.

HEALTHNUT TIP Check the label when buying nuts, seeds, and dried coconut to make sure there is no added sugar or hydrogenated oils, because we don't have time for that nonsense.

Lemon Herb White Bean Hummus

Makes 2 cups • **Prep Time 10 minutes**

Ingredients

¼ cup tahini

2 cloves garlic, chopped

Zest and juice of 1 lemon

1 can (19 ounces/540 mL) cannellini
    beans, rinsed and drained (or
    2 cups cooked cannellini beans)

3 tablespoons water

2 tablespoons extra-virgin olive oil

½ teaspoon sea salt

¼ teaspoon pepper

1 tablespoon chopped fresh chives

1 tablespoon chopped fresh thyme

1 tablespoon chopped fresh
    rosemary

For this yummy hummus, I use cannellini beans (a.k.a. white kidney beans) instead of the traditional chickpeas to create the most creamy and smooth dip or spread for anything you would use regular hummus for. The flavour is light and allows the lemon and fresh herbs to really shine through in every bite. This is great for dipping raw veggies into, or serve with crackers or warm pita bread, or use as a spread on my Mushrooms on Toast (page 141).

1. Put the tahini, garlic, and lemon juice in a food processor and process for 2 minutes until creamy and smooth. Add the beans, lemon zest, water, olive oil, salt, and pepper. Process for 2 to 3 minutes, until creamy and smooth, stopping halfway through to scrape down the sides. Add the chives, thyme, and rosemary and process for 30 seconds.

2. Serve immediately, or store in an airtight container in the fridge for 2 hours to let the flavours blend and allow the hummus to firm up. Store any leftovers in an airtight container in the fridge for up to 5 days.

🌰 **HEALTHNUT TIP** If you don't have fresh herbs on hand, you can use dried herbs. Since dried herbs are more concentrated, use 1 teaspoon of each.

Beet Goat Cheese Hummus

Makes 2 cups • **Prep Time 15 minutes** • **Cook Time 25 to 30 minutes**

Ingredients

3 small red beets, peeled and
    cut into ½-inch cubes (about
    1½ cups)
1 teaspoon avocado oil
¼ cup tahini
2 cloves garlic, chopped
Juice of 1 small lemon
1 can (14 ounces/398 mL)
    chickpeas, rinsed and drained
    (or 1½ cups cooked chickpeas)
¼ cup water
2 tablespoons extra-virgin olive oil
½ teaspoon sea salt
¼ teaspoon pepper
¼ cup soft goat cheese

Garnishes

2 tablespoons crumbled goat
    cheese
2 tablespoons chopped pitted
    Kalamata olives

The first time I ever had beet hummus was at a friend's housewarming party in Perth, Australia. It was a couple of years before I started seeing it in stores across Canada, and now every time I taste it I think of my travels and how cool it is that recipes and flavours make their way across the world. This hummus is flavourful with a beautiful hue of colour from the beets, and perfect as an appetizer for parties. Serve with raw veggies, crackers, or warm pita bread, or spread on toasted sourdough, or use in my Falafel Mediterranean Bowl (page 148).

1. Preheat the oven to 450°F. Drape a large sheet of foil over a baking sheet.

2. Place the beet cubes on the foil. Drizzle with the avocado oil, sprinkle with salt and pepper to taste, and toss to coat well. Fold in the sides of the foil, fold over the top, and seal tightly to create a foil packet. This will keep the steam in and allow the beets to cook faster. Roast for 25 to 30 minutes, or until the beets are fork-tender. Remove from the oven, open the foil packet, and allow the beets to cool slightly.

3. Put the tahini, garlic, and lemon juice in a food processor and process for 2 minutes, until creamy and smooth. Add the roasted beets, chickpeas, water, olive oil, salt, and pepper. Process for 2 to 3 minutes, until creamy and smooth, stopping halfway through to scrape down the sides. Add the goat cheese and process for another 30 seconds.

4. Serve immediately, topped with crumbled goat cheese and olives, or store in an airtight container in the fridge for 2 hours to let the flavours blend and for the hummus to firm up, then garnish with goat cheese and olives just before serving. Store any leftovers in an airtight container in the fridge for up to 5 days.

🥜 **HEALTHNUT TIP** If you are short on time, you can find vacuum-sealed precooked beets in the refrigerated section at the grocery store. Another option is to roast up a large batch of beets during your weekend meal prep; use some for the hummus and add the rest to salads or nourish bowls.

Turmeric Tahini Hummus

Makes 2 cups • **Prep Time 10 minutes**

Ingredients

¼ cup tahini

2 cloves garlic, chopped

Juice of 1 lemon

1 can (19 ounces/540 mL)
   chickpeas, rinsed and drained
   (or 2 cups cooked chickpeas)

¼ cup water

2 tablespoons extra-virgin olive oil

½ teaspoon ground turmeric

½ teaspoon sea salt

¼ teaspoon pepper

1½ teaspoons sesame seeds,
   for garnish

I love eating the rainbow when it comes to foods, so giving my go-to basic hummus a golden makeover tricks my mind into thinking I'm eating something fun and new. With its beautiful hue of golden yellow, turmeric is an amazing anti-inflammatory food. This hummus pairs well with my Rosemary and Sea Salt Almond Crackers (page 88) or sliced cucumber and radish, or go the traditional route with crackers or warm pita bread. Whether you spread or dip, you'll love this traditional hummus with a flair.

1. Put the tahini, garlic, and lemon juice in a food processor and process for 2 minutes, until creamy and smooth. Add the chickpeas, water, olive oil, turmeric, salt, and pepper. Process for 2 to 3 minutes, until creamy and smooth, stopping halfway through to scrape down the sides.

2. Serve immediately, garnished with sesame seeds, or store in an airtight container in the fridge for 2 hours to let the flavours blend and for the hummus to firm up. Store any leftovers in an airtight container in the fridge for up to 5 days.

Not-So-Basic Guacamole

Makes 1½ cups • Prep Time 10 minutes

Ingredients

2 large ripe avocados

Juice of 1 lime

1 clove garlic, minced

½ jalapeño pepper, seeded and
   finely chopped

¼ cup finely chopped red onion

¼ cup fresh cilantro, chopped

¼ teaspoon ground cumin

¼ teaspoon sea salt

¼ teaspoon pepper

I'm all about that guac life. This is my go-to appetizer for parties, potlucks, or late-night munchies with a bowl of blue corn chips. Not only is guacamole super tasty with its zesty, creamy, and fresh flavour, but you can feel good knowing you're hydrating your body and getting some healthy fats, protein, and fibre with every dip! I personally like to enjoy my guac on the chunky side, but however you mash it up, it will be better than store-bought every time. Best served right away with corn chips, cut raw veggies, or as a side for my Cheesy Bean Loaded Nachos (page 87).

1. Cut the avocados in half lengthwise, twist, remove the pit, and using a spoon, scoop the flesh into a medium bowl. Sprinkle the lime juice over the avocado and mash with a fork or potato masher to desired consistency.

2. Add the garlic, jalapeño, onions, cilantro, cumin, salt, and pepper and mix. Serve right away!

🌰 **HEALTHNUT TIP** Avocado oxidizes quickly, so I recommend making guacamole just before serving. If you like your guacamole chilled, make it with ripe avocados that have been refrigerated overnight.

Popcorn Three Ways

Makes 4 to 5 cups • Prep Time 5 minutes

When movie night comes around, there's nothing I love more than snacking on a big bowl of freshly popped popcorn. It has got to be the easiest and cheapest snack to make when you're feeling peckish but it's too late to eat a whole meal. I keep a container of organic popcorn in the cupboard at all times, just in case. The hardest part is deciding what to top it with, so I'm sharing my favourite three flavours to help you out. Now all you'll have to figure out is the best way to sneak this into the movie theatre!

Basic Popcorn

Ingredients

1 tablespoon coconut oil
½ cup organic popcorn kernels

1. In a large pot over medium-high heat, melt the coconut oil. Add 2 popcorn kernels, cover, and let sit until they pop, indicating the oil is hot enough. Remove the popped kernels. Add the remaining popcorn kernels, cover, and shake the pot to fully coat them in oil.

2. Keep the pot covered and shake the pot every so often until kernels start to pop. Continue to shake as the popcorn pops to prevent burning. Once the popping noises slow down to one pop every 2 or 3 seconds, remove from the heat and let rest for several seconds to allow any last pops. Transfer the popcorn to a large bowl.

Old Bay Classic

Ingredients

1 batch Basic Popcorn
1 tablespoon nutritional yeast
1 teaspoon Old Bay seasoning
½ teaspoon garlic powder
¼ teaspoon sea salt
¼ teaspoon pepper
1 to 2 tablespoons coconut oil, melted

1. Make the Basic Popcorn according to the instructions.

2. While the popcorn is popping, in a small bowl, stir together the nutritional yeast, Old Bay seasoning, garlic powder, salt, and pepper.

3. Drizzle the popcorn with the desired amount of melted coconut oil, then sprinkle with the seasoning mixture. Using your hands, gently toss to evenly coat the popcorn and enjoy.

Salted Caramel Peanut

Prep Ahead
Salted Caramel Butter (page 233)

Ingredients
1 batch Basic Popcorn
½ cup whole redskin peanuts
1 batch Salted Caramel Butter,
   warmed

1. Make the Basic Popcorn according to the instructions.

2. Line 2 baking sheets with parchment paper and spread out the popcorn. Sprinkle evenly with peanuts. Drizzle with Salted Caramel Butter. Let set for 5 to 10 minutes, then transfer back to a large bowl and enjoy.

Cheesy Dill

Ingredients
1 batch Basic Popcorn
2 tablespoons nutritional yeast
2 teaspoons dried dill
½ teaspoon garlic powder
½ teaspoon sea salt
1 to 2 tablespoons coconut oil,
   melted

1. Make the Basic Popcorn according to the instructions.

2. While the popcorn is popping, in a small bowl, stir together the nutritional yeast, dill, garlic powder, and salt.

3. Drizzle the popcorn with the desired amount of coconut oil, then sprinkle with the seasoning mixture. Using your hands, gently toss to evenly coat the popcorn and enjoy.

Cheesy Bean Loaded Nachos

Serves 4 to 6 • **Prep Time 10 minutes** • **Bake Time 5 minutes**

Prep Ahead

Maple "Baked" Beans (page 183)

Nacho Average Cheese Sauce
  (page 226)

Quick Pickled Red Onions (page 224)

Not-So-Basic Guacamole (page 82)

Ingredients

2 cups Maple "Baked" Beans or
  canned maple baked beans

½ cup Nacho Average Cheese
  Sauce

1 bag (10½ ounces/300 g)
  tortilla corn chips

½ cup medium hot salsa

Quick Pickled Red Onions, for
  garnish

Chopped fresh cilantro, for garnish

Not-So-Basic Guacamole (optional)

Cheesy, messy loaded nachos. Yes, these are as good as they look and sound! I'm often asked if I ever sit down to a plate of wings or nachos, and the answer is always "Yes, of course!" That said, if I can make them at home in my own healthified way using fresh, homemade ingredients, then you bet that's what I'm going to do. It's all about balance, and sometimes life calls for guilt-free drinks and nachos with family and friends on a weekend afternoon!

1. Preheat the broiler.

2. Meanwhile, reheat the Maple "Baked" Beans and Nacho Average Cheese Sauce.

3. Spread the tortilla chips on a baking sheet and broil for 5 minutes or until warm. Top the tortilla chips with the beans, cheese sauce, and salsa. Garnish with Quick Pickled Red Onions and cilantro. Enjoy with a side of Not-So-Basic Guacamole, if desired.

VARIATION For a non-vegetarian version, use crumbled leftover Apple Maple Breakfast Sausage Patties (page 59) in place of the beans. For a different flavour combination, substitute pickled jalapeños for pickled onions and pico de gallo in place of the salsa.

Rosemary and Sea Salt Almond Crackers

Makes 40 crackers • **Prep Time 10 minutes** • **Bake Time 20 to 22 minutes**

Ingredients

1 cup almond flour

¼ cup oat flour

1 tablespoon ground flaxseed

1 tablespoon nutritional yeast

1 teaspoon dried rosemary

¼ teaspoon garlic powder

¼ teaspoon baking powder

¼ teaspoon sea salt

1 egg

1 tablespoon extra-virgin olive oil

Toppings

1 tablespoon extra-virgin olive oil

1 teaspoon dried rosemary

1 teaspoon sea salt

VARIATION Instead of rosemary, use sesame seeds, caraway seeds, or everything bagel seasoning.

🌰 **HEALTHNUT TIP** If you don't have almond flour, a kitchen hack is to grind some blanched almonds (whole, slivered, or sliced) in the food processor for about 10 seconds for a cheap and quick almond flour on demand.

Making your own crackers might seem like a tedious, time-consuming thing to do, but these crispy almond crackers are super simple to whip up and taste far superior to anything from the store. The fun part is you can flavour them differently each time, using your favourite herbs and spices so you'll never get bored. These gluten-free, wholesome, protein-packed crackers are great for dipping in my Turmeric Tahini Hummus (page 81) or Creamy Leek and Potato Soup (page 161).

1. Preheat the oven to 350°F.

2. In a medium bowl, stir together the almond flour, oat flour, flaxseed, nutritional yeast, rosemary, garlic powder, baking powder, and salt.

3. Make a well in the centre, crack in the egg, and pour in the olive oil. Stir everything together until a smooth dough forms. Using your hands, shape the dough into a ball.

4. Place the dough between 2 sheets of parchment paper and roll it out into a large rectangle ⅛ inch thick, rolling from the centre outwards in all directions. Remove the top sheet of parchment paper and, using a pizza cutter, trim the edges of the dough to form clean, straight lines, setting aside the edges. Using the pizza cutter, cut the rectangle into 1-inch squares, but do not separate them. Slide the dough on the bottom parchment paper onto a baking sheet. Freeze for about 5 minutes to firm up the dough, making them easier to handle when separating them.

5. While the crackers are in the freezer, roll the trimmed edges into a ball. Roll out and cut the dough the same way, then transfer to another baking sheet and freeze for about 5 minutes.

6. Remove the chilled dough from the freezer and separate the crackers with your fingers, leaving ¼ inch between each cracker. Brush the crackers with half of the olive oil and sprinkle with half of the rosemary and salt. Bake for 10 to 11 minutes, until the edges are slightly golden. Repeat with the second sheet of chilled dough.

7. Slide the crackers on the parchment paper onto a rack and let cool completely. Store in an airtight container at room temperature for up to 1 week or in a resealable freezer bag in the freezer for up to 1 month.

Everyday Nut and Seed Loaf

Makes 1 loaf • Prep Time 5 minutes • Bake Time 25 to 30 minutes

Ingredients

1½ cups almond flour

3 tablespoons ground flaxseed

2 tablespoons coconut flour

1½ teaspoons baking powder

½ teaspoon sea salt

4 eggs

2 tablespoons coconut oil, melted, plus more for the pan

1 tablespoon pure liquid honey

Toppings

1½ teaspoons raw pumpkin seeds

1½ teaspoons raw sunflower seeds

1½ teaspoons chia seeds

1½ teaspoons whole flax seeds

Variations of this nut and seed loaf have been a go-to staple for me. I love stocking my freezer with slices that are ready to pop in the toaster for breakfast with some mashed avocado, or as a sweet afternoon treat with my Vanilla Roasted Almond Butter (page 228) and fresh raspberries. Whether enjoyed sweet or savoury, morning or afternoon, this protein- and fibre-packed loaf is filled with healthful ingredients to give you the kick of energy you need to get through your day.

1. Preheat the oven to 350°F. Line a 9- x 5-inch loaf pan with parchment paper, leaving the edges hanging over for easy lifting once baked, and grease lightly with coconut oil.

2. In a large bowl, combine the almond flour, ground flaxseed, coconut flour, baking powder, and salt. Make a well in the centre and crack in the eggs. Add the coconut oil and honey. Stir just until the mixture is moist and thick. You're looking for a thick batter but not a dough.

3. Scrape the batter into the loaf pan and smooth the top with a spatula so it bakes evenly. Sprinkle with the pumpkin seeds, sunflower seeds, chia seeds, and whole flax seeds. Gently press the seeds into the batter to help them stick. Bake for 25 to 30 minutes until the top and edges are slightly golden and a toothpick inserted in the centre comes out clean.

4. Let cool in the pan for 5 minutes. Lift the loaf from the pan and transfer to a rack and let cool completely before slicing. Store in an airtight container at room temperature for up to 3 days or in the fridge for up to 1 week.

VARIATION For a sweeter loaf, add 2 teaspoons of cinnamon to the flour mixture. Drizzle the top with 1 tablespoon of honey before baking.

Chewy Trail Mix Granola Bars

Makes 10 bars • **Prep Time 10 minutes** • **Cook Time 15 minutes**

Ingredients

2 cups old-fashioned rolled oats

1 cup whole raw almonds

10 Medjool dates, pitted

½ cup pure maple syrup

⅓ cup natural peanut butter

1 teaspoon pure vanilla extract

½ cup raw pumpkin seeds

½ cup hemp hearts

½ teaspoon cinnamon

¼ teaspoon sea salt (omit if
  using salted peanut butter)

I may be biased, but these are the best granola bars ever! They are loved by so many of my HealthNut foodies around the world. Hearty, chewy, and naturally sweetened, these bars are loaded with toasted oats and almonds, and are held together by a sticky date and peanut butter caramel for the perfect salty-sweet crunch in every bite. I take these on road trips, hiking, camping—basically anywhere I want a portable healthy snack that will keep me fuelled and energized.

1. Preheat the oven to 350°F. Line a baking sheet with parchment paper. Line an 8-inch square baking pan with parchment paper long enough to fold over the edges.

2. Mix together the oats and almonds on the baking sheet and lightly toast for 10 minutes, stirring halfway through. Transfer to a large bowl and set aside.

3. In a food processor, process the dates until they are smooth and form a ball of "date dough." Leave the dates in the food processor.

4. In a small saucepan, combine the maple syrup, peanut butter, and vanilla. Heat over medium-low heat for 1 to 2 minutes, stirring, until the mixture is melted and has a caramel-like texture. Pour into the food processor with the date dough and process for 15 seconds, or until smooth.

5. To the toasted oat and almond mixture, add the pumpkin seeds, hemp hearts, cinnamon, and salt, if using. Give it a quick stir to combine. Scrape in the caramel date mixture and stir with a wooden spoon (it won't stick as much) until well combined. I like to use my hands, but be careful—the caramel can still be hot, so let it cool slightly so you don't burn yourself.

6. Scrape the mixture into the prepared baking pan, pressing down firmly with the bottom of a cup or jar to compress the mixture. Cover and refrigerate for 30 minutes to allow it to harden.

7. Lift from the pan and cut into 10 even bars. Store the granola bars in an airtight container at room temperature for up to 5 days, in the fridge for up to 1 week, or in the freezer for up to 1 month.

Oatmeal Raisin Cookie Energy Bites

Makes 18 to 20 bites • Prep Time 10 minutes • Chill Time 15 minutes

Ingredients

1½ cups old-fashioned rolled oats

½ cup whole raw walnuts

¾ teaspoon cinnamon

Sea salt

⅓ cup unsweetened shredded coconut

½ cup natural almond butter

⅓ cup pure maple syrup

½ cup Thompson raisins

Your traditional oatmeal raisin cookie just got turned into grab-and-go energy bites that are perfect as a pre- or post-workout snack, afternoon pick-me-up, or cheeky late-night dessert. Sweet, oaty, and nutty, with a warming touch of cinnamon, and so easy to pulse up in your food processor for a no-bake energizing snack. Now, if only I could dip these in almond milk like a regular cookie, I would be all set.

1. In a food processor, combine the oats, walnuts, cinnamon, and a pinch of salt; pulse for 15 to 30 seconds until crumbly. Add the shredded coconut and pulse for 5 seconds to blend together.

2. Transfer the oat mixture to a large bowl and add the almond butter and maple syrup. Stir with a spatula until well combined. Fold in the raisins.

3. Line a baking sheet with parchment paper. Using your hands, shape about 2 tablespoons of the mixture at a time into balls and place on the baking sheet.

4. Refrigerate the balls for 15 to 30 minutes, until hardened. You can enjoy them straight away or store in an airtight container at room temperature for up to 5 days, in the fridge for up to 1 week, or in the freezer for up to 1 month.

🌰 **HEALTHNUT TIP** Store in an airtight container in the freezer so you always have these handy to pop into your lunch box, or as you run out the door for a morning sweat at the gym.

Golden Milk Latte Smoothie

Serves 1 to 2 • Prep Time 5 minutes

....

Prep Ahead

Steamed and Frozen Butternut
Squash (see page 223)

Ingredients

1½ cups unsweetened coconut milk
(from the carton)

1 cup Steamed and Frozen Butternut
Squash

1 frozen ripe medium banana

1 tablespoon natural almond butter

1 teaspoon grated peeled fresh
ginger

½ teaspoon ground turmeric
(or 1 teaspoon grated peeled
fresh turmeric)

½ teaspoon cinnamon

Pepper

Optional Boosters

1 scoop vanilla plant-based protein
powder

1 tablespoon hemp hearts

1 tablespoon ground flaxseed

1 tablespoon grass-fed collagen
powder

Soothing, comforting, and healing, this smoothie has the superpowers of turmeric while providing the warm, spiced flavour of a golden milk latte. I love the slight kick you get from the ginger and black pepper, and it pairs perfectly with the creamy coconut milk and banana base. I like to make this smoothie in the fall and winter months when squash and pumpkin are in season and to keep me warm with all those warming spices.

1. In a high-speed blender, combine the coconut milk, butternut squash, banana, almond butter, ginger, turmeric, cinnamon, and a pinch of pepper. Add 1 or 2 boosters for extra protein and fibre. Blend on high speed for 1 minute or until smooth.

Iced Dirty Chai "Coffee" on the Rocks

Serves 1 • Prep Time 5 minutes

Prep Ahead

Chai Cashew Milk (page 100)

Ingredients

½ to 1 cup ice cubes

¾ cup brewed herbal or
   regular coffee, cooled

⅓ cup Chai Cashew Milk

I don't drink coffee, so I only recently found out what a dirty chai latte is (shocking, I know). I was immediately intrigued! As usual, I decided to make my own version, using my creamy Chai Cashew Milk over ice with cold-brew herbal coffee. This drink is so good that you'll be making those slurpy noises with your straw as you reach the bottom of your glass. Of course you can make this iced latte with your regular cup of joe—either way, I know it will become your new favourite coffee. All you need is a sunny day and a good book to chill with while you sip and cool off, because you deserve it.

1. In a tall glass filled with ice, add the coffee and Chai Cashew Milk. Stir and enjoy!

VARIATION You can make this drink with real coffee, rooibos, black tea, or even with a scoop of cacao powder for a mocha chocolaty option.

Pink Latte

Makes 2 cups • Prep Time 5 minutes • Cook Time 10 minutes

Ingredients

2 cups unsweetened coconut milk
(from the carton)

1½ teaspoons to 1 tablespoon pure
liquid honey

1 teaspoon grated peeled fresh
ginger

1 cinnamon stick

Sea salt

1 tablespoon grated raw red beet

1 teaspoon ghee

Ground nutmeg

Golden milk lattes have officially met their match with this super-cute and Instagram-worthy pink latte. As someone who doesn't drink coffee, I'm always looking for ways to enjoy a hot, frothy beverage without the caffeine. And even if you're a coffee lover, sometimes it's nice to switch it up, take a break in the afternoon, or enjoy a nice nightcap with something warm, soothing, and comforting.

1. In a small saucepan, combine the coconut milk, 1½ teaspoons of the honey, ginger, cinnamon stick, and a pinch of salt. Bring to a boil over medium heat. Reduce the heat and simmer for 10 minutes, whisking frequently to prevent the milk from burning. Remove from the heat.

2. Wearing rubber gloves to prevent staining your hands, squeeze the beet over the saucepan to release the juice. Discard the pulp. Taste and add more honey, if desired.

3. Remove the cinnamon stick and transfer the liquid to a high-speed blender. Add the ghee and blend on high speed for 30 seconds. Pour into 2 cups and sprinkle with a pinch of nutmeg.

🌰 **HEALTHNUT TIP** Depending on the freshness of your beet, you may get less or more juice out of the grated pulp.

Chai Cashew Milk

Makes 4 cups • Soak Time 4 to 6 hours or overnight • Prep Time 5 minutes

Ingredients

1 cup raw cashews

3½ cups water

1 teaspoon pure vanilla extract

2 Medjool dates, pitted

1 teaspoon cinnamon

¼ teaspoon ground ginger

¼ teaspoon sea salt

Ground cardamom

Ground allspice

Ground nutmeg

Store-bought nut and seed milks are convenient, but nothing compares with the freshly blended homemade version. This cashew milk is so creamy and delicious, you'll never guess it's dairy-free. The best part about cashew milk is that it doesn't require any straining through a nut milk bag to separate the pulp. As long as you have a high-speed blender, it's a breeze to whip up any time. I've been experimenting with various flavourings, and I'm currently in love with the invigorating spices of chai. Best enjoyed with my Almond Swirl Chocolate Brownies (page 193) or as a base for my Iced Dirty Chai "Coffee" on the Rocks (page 97).

1. Soak the cashews in enough water to cover for 4 to 6 hours or overnight.

2. Drain and rinse the cashews and transfer them to a high-speed blender. Add the water, vanilla, dates, cinnamon, ginger, salt, and a pinch each of cardamom, allspice, and nutmeg. Blend on high speed for 1 to 2 minutes until creamy. The milk will be creamy, but you can add ½ to 1 cup more water for a consistency like 1% milk.

3. Serve chilled over ice or warmed. Transfer any leftovers to a glass bottle with a lid and store in the fridge for up to 3 days.

🌰 **HEALTHNUT TIP** Forgot to soak your cashews? Submerge the raw cashews in a small bowl of boiling water for 15 minutes to get them soft and ready for blending.

Blueberry Basil Smoothie

Serves 1 to 2 • **Prep Time 5 minutes**

Prep Ahead

Steamed and Frozen Cauliflower
Florets (see page 223)

Ingredients

1½ cups unsweetened coconut milk
(from the carton)

1 cup Steamed and Frozen
Cauliflower Florets

½ frozen ripe medium banana

½ cup frozen blueberries

1 tablespoon natural almond butter

4 or 5 fresh basil leaves

¼ teaspoon cinnamon

Optional Boosters

1 scoop vanilla plant-based protein
powder

1 tablespoon hemp hearts

1 tablespoon ground flaxseed

1 tablespoon grass-fed collagen
powder

Smoothies are my go-to weekday breakfast, so since I drink a lot of them, I love having fun creating new flavour combinations with what's in the fridge—or in this case, garden. The slight hint of fresh basil gives this smoothie an aromatic sweet but savoury feel that pairs perfectly with the burst of mellow tart sweetness from the berries and hidden veggie. Usually when you think of fresh herbs in a drink, it's a happy-hour cocktail! But hey, it's fun to switch things up, and this purple smoothie is suitable for all occasions.

1. In a high-speed blender, combine the coconut milk, cauliflower, banana, blueberries, almond butter, basil, and cinnamon. Add 1 or 2 boosters for extra protein and fibre. Blend on high speed for 1 minute or until smooth.

VARIATION For a lighter and more hydrating option, I like to use a combo of half water, half milk in my smoothies.

Pineapple Green Dream Smoothie

Serves 1 to 2 • **Prep Time 5 minutes**

Ingredients

½ cup cold water

½ cup unsweetened almond milk
or coconut milk (from the carton)

1 to 2 cups loosely packed baby
spinach

½ English cucumber, roughly
chopped

½ cup frozen pineapple chunks

½ frozen ripe medium banana

4 or 5 fresh mint leaves

3 ice cubes

Optional Boosters

1 scoop vanilla plant-based protein
powder

1 tablespoon hemp hearts

1 tablespoon ground flaxseed

1 tablespoon grass-fed collagen
powder

This is the smoothie to make for someone new to the world of green smoothies. The fresh pineapple zing and creamy banana are the perfect base to mask the spinach—the only way you'll know it's in there is from the distinct green hue. The cucumber makes this smoothie super hydrating, so think of it as "food for your skin, from within" because I firmly believe food is the best type of skincare for making your skin glow. Add a scoop of protein powder for an energizing breakfast or drink as a mid-afternoon pick-me-up.

1. In a high-speed blender, combine the water, almond milk, spinach, cucumber, pineapple, banana, mint, and ice cubes. Add 1 or 2 boosters for extra protein and fibre. Blend on high speed for 1 minute or until smooth.

Malibu Sunrise Smoothie

Serves 1 to 2 • **Prep Time 5 minutes**

Prep Ahead

Steamed and Frozen Butternut
Squash (see page 223)

Ingredients

1½ cups unsweetened coconut milk
(from the carton)

Juice of ½ lemon

½ cup frozen raspberries

½ cup frozen strawberries

1 orange, peeled and seeded

1 cup Steamed and Frozen Butternut
Squash

½ frozen ripe medium banana

Optional Boosters

1 scoop vanilla plant-based protein
powder

1 tablespoon hemp hearts

1 tablespoon ground flaxseed

1 tablespoon grass-fed collagen
powder

This tropical treat blended with mixed berries and citrus provides a naturally sweetened and tangy burst of flavour. I love whipping up this drink when I'm over my green smoothies and feel like something both pleasing to the eye and nutrient dense. Besides, when your smoothie is this pretty, no one will know there are veggies hidden inside.

1. In a high-speed blender, combine the coconut milk, lemon juice, raspberries, strawberries, orange, butternut squash, and banana. Add 1 or 2 boosters for extra protein and fibre. Blend on high speed for 1 minute or until smooth.

Everyday Green Smoothie

Serves 1 to 2 • **Prep Time 5 minutes**

Ingredients

½ cup unsweetened almond milk or
coconut milk (from the carton)

½ cup water

Juice of ½ lime

1 frozen ripe medium banana

½ English cucumber, chopped

2 handfuls baby spinach

1 Medjool date, pitted

¼ cup fresh flat-leaf parsley

1 tablespoon natural almond butter

1½ teaspoons hemp oil

¼ teaspoon Hawaiian spirulina
powder

¼ teaspoon cinnamon

3 ice cubes

Optional Boosters

1 scoop vanilla plant-based protein
powder

1 tablespoon hemp hearts

1 tablespoon ground flaxseed

1 tablespoon grass-fed collagen
powder

I still remember the first time I discovered the genius idea of disguising greens in a smoothie. I'm not going to lie, I was originally very skeptical—a salad in my smoothie cup? It was my roommate back in college who introduced me to it all by sharing his three-ingredient recipe: banana, romaine lettuce, blueberries, and water. I had a taste and was forever hooked! My green smoothies have come a long way since then and are now my "morning liquid multivitamin."

1. In a high-speed blender, combine the almond milk, water, lime juice, banana, cucumber, spinach, date, parsley, almond butter, hemp oil, spirulina, cinnamon, and ice cubes. Add 1 or 2 boosters for extra protein and fibre. Blend on high speed for 1 minute or until smooth.

HEALTHNUT TIP Spirulina powder is a blue-green algae that is high in plant protein, antioxidants, and B vitamins. It also helps remove heavy metals from the body. I always buy Hawaiian spirulina because it is higher in quality and doesn't have a strong fishy taste or scent.

Piña Colada Smoothie Bowl

Serves 2 to 3 • Prep Time 5 minutes

Prep Ahead

Steamed and Frozen Cauliflower
Florets (see page 223)

No-Bake Coconut Almond Clusters
(page 76)

Ingredients

1¼ cups unsweetened coconut milk
(from the carton)

Juice of 1 lime

2 frozen ripe medium bananas,
roughly chopped

1 cup Steamed and Frozen
Cauliflower Florets

1 cup frozen pineapple chunks

¼ teaspoon ground turmeric

Optional Boosters

1 scoop vanilla plant-based protein
powder

1 tablespoon hemp hearts

1 tablespoon ground flaxseed

1 tablespoon grass-fed collagen
powder

Toppings

½ cup No-Bake Coconut Almond
Clusters

Fresh cherries

Unsweetened coconut flakes

Dried pineapple (optional)

How can anyone say "piña colada" without turning it into a song?
"I love piña coladas and (not so much) getting caught in the rain!"
My non-alcoholic version, blended up into a thick and creamy smoothie
bowl, and loaded with toppings for a stunning look, is mouth-watering
with a burst of zing from the lime. Not to mention that smoothies are
just more fun to enjoy with a spoon!

1. In a high-speed blender, combine the coconut milk, lime juice, bananas,
   cauliflower, pineapple, and turmeric. Add 1 or 2 boosters for extra
   protein and fibre. Blend on high speed for 1 minute or until smooth.

2. Serve in a bowl topped with crumbled No-Bake Coconut Almond
   Clusters, cherries, coconut flakes, and dried pineapple, if using.

Easy Blender Green Juice

Serves 2 • **Prep Time 10 minutes**

Ingredients

2 kale leaves, roughly torn

2 Swiss chard leaves, roughly torn

¼ cup fresh flat-leaf parsley leaves

4 to 6 fresh mint leaves

1 Granny Smith apple, cored and
  roughly chopped

½ English cucumber, roughly
  chopped

1 cup fresh pineapple chunks

½-inch piece fresh ginger

Juice of 1 lemon

1 cup water

I used to have a juicer until I discovered that I could easily make fresh fruit and veggie juices right in my blender and strain out the pulp using some cheesecloth or my trusty nut milk bag. I'm not missing my old juicer at all—or the cleanup! This green juice is loaded with vitamins and minerals. Enjoy it first thing in the morning on an empty stomach to hydrate and wake up your body or throughout the day as a refreshing, revitalizing drink.

1. In a high-speed blender, combine the kale, Swiss chard, parsley, mint, apple, cucumber, pineapple, ginger, lemon juice, and water. Blend on high speed for 1 minute or until smooth.

2. Strain the juice through a nut milk bag or a double layer of cheesecloth into a large bowl. Squeeze the bag until you are left with a semi-dry pulp.

3. Pour into glasses and serve as is or over ice. Store any leftovers in a glass jar in the fridge for up to 2 days or in the freezer for up to 2 weeks. Transfer to fridge the day before to thaw before drinking.

SALADS

Fennel Citrus Kale Salad

Serves 4 • Prep Time 15 minutes

Orange Basil Mint Vinaigrette

Zest of 1 orange

Juice of ½ orange

Juice of ½ lemon

3 tablespoons extra-virgin olive oil

1 tablespoon apple cider vinegar

1 tablespoon finely chopped
    fresh basil

1 tablespoon finely chopped
    fresh mint

Sea salt and pepper

Fennel Citrus Kale Salad

4 cups packed stemmed and
    thinly sliced black kale

1 tablespoon fresh lemon juice

1½ teaspoons extra-virgin olive oil

Sea salt

2 cups thinly sliced fennel
    (about 1 small fennel bulb)

1 cup thinly sliced radishes
    (about 5 radishes)

½ cup thinly sliced red onion

1 orange, peeled and segmented

1 Granny Smith apple, sliced into
    matchsticks

This salad is almost too pretty to eat. It is fresh, crunchy, sweet, and citrusy, and the flavour just gets better as it marinates in the dressing. I had always assumed I wouldn't like fennel, as it has a slight licorice flavour and I've never been a fan of licorice candy. But surprisingly it has become a new favourite in my kitchen, and I love enjoying it sautéed, roasted, or raw in salads like this one. It gives salads a bright taste and really adds a depth of unexpected flavour that cleanses and refreshes your palate.

1. **Make the Orange Basil Mint Vinaigrette** In a glass jar, combine the orange zest, orange juice, lemon juice, olive oil, cider vinegar, basil, mint, and a pinch each of salt and pepper. Cover and shake until well combined.

2. **Prepare the Fennel Citrus Kale Salad** In a large salad bowl, combine the kale, lemon juice, olive oil, and a pinch of salt. Massage the kale with your hands for about 30 seconds to soften. Add the fennel, radishes, onion, orange, and apple. Toss well.

3. Pour the vinaigrette over the salad, toss again, and serve. Salad will keep in an airtight container in the fridge for up to 2 days with the dressing or up to 4 days without the dressing.

VARIATION For a complete healthy and filling lunch or dinner, serve with grilled chicken, salmon, or tofu.

🌰 **HEALTHNUT TIP** The key to this salad is thinly slicing all the veggies, which I like to use my handy mandoline slicer for. Just make sure you use the provided guard to protect your fingers.

Green Bean Salad with Grated Beet

Serves 4 • Prep Time 10 minutes • Cook Time 5 minutes

Dijon Vinaigrette

1 clove garlic, minced

⅓ cup extra-virgin olive oil

2 tablespoons balsamic vinegar

1 tablespoon grainy Dijon mustard

Sea salt and pepper

Green Bean Salad with Grated Beet

1 pound (450 g) French green
   beans, trimmed

⅓ cup sliced blanched almonds

1 large raw red beet, peeled and
   grated

2 tablespoons Almond Flour Parm
   (page 225)

There are two types of green bean eaters in this world—those who like them bright green and crunchy, and those who like them soft and overcooked (i.e., dead). Can you guess which one I am? You guessed it—crunchy all the way, and this salad is just that. The grated raw beet and Dijon Vinaigrette will change your relationship with green veggies from "it's complicated" to "in a committed relationship." Besides, who said salads had to be all leafy greens? The definition of a salad is a mixture of raw or cooked vegetables, usually seasoned with oil and vinegar, so this is indeed a salad.

1. **Make the Dijon Vinaigrette** In a small jar, combine the garlic, olive oil, balsamic vinegar, mustard, and a pinch each of salt and pepper. Cover and shake well until emulsified.

2. **Prepare the Green Bean Salad with Grated Beet** Blanch the green beans in a medium saucepan of salted boiling water for 5 minutes. Drain and transfer to a large bowl filled with ice water.

3. Toast the sliced almonds in a skillet over medium heat for 3 to 4 minutes, until lightly golden brown, stirring frequently.

4. Drain the green beans and pat dry. In a large bowl, toss the beans with the desired amount of Dijon Vinaigrette. Top with the grated beet, toasted almonds, and Almond Flour Parm, and serve immediately. Salad will keep in an airtight container in the fridge for up to 2 days with the dressing or up to 4 days without the dressing.

🌰 **HEALTHNUT TIP** If you're making this for your weekly meal prep, store the almonds, Almond Flour Parm, and dressing on the side to add fresh when you're ready to eat. You can store the dressing in the jar in the fridge for up to 5 days. Reshake before using.

Gigi's Warm Black-Eyed Pea Salad

Serves 4 to 6 • Prep Time 5 minute • Cook Time 20 minutes

Prep Ahead

Jammy Eggs (page 218)

Ingredients

1 pound (450 g) mini red potatoes, quartered

1 can (19 ounces/540 mL) black-eyed peas, rinsed and drained (or 2 cups cooked black-eyed peas)

½ red onion, thinly sliced into rings

½ cup pitted black olives

4 Jammy Eggs, sliced in half lengthwise

Classic Oil and Vinegar Dressing

⅓ cup extra-virgin olive oil

¼ cup fresh flat-leaf parsley, finely chopped

1 clove garlic, minced

2 tablespoons red wine vinegar

1 teaspoon grainy Dijon mustard

Sea salt and pepper

In case you're wondering, Gigi (short for Grandma Grace) is the nickname I gave my mom when my nephew, Orrin, was born. This is a simple Portuguese-style salad made up of beans, eggs, red onion, black olives—ingredients you likely already have on hand—and a basic vinaigrette that my mom makes all the time. I say "Portuguese-style," but really, I call anything my parents make "Portuguese-style"—even if it's pizza and fries. You can pair this salad with roasted chicken or fish, but it's hearty enough to enjoy on its own.

1. Put the potatoes in a large pot of salted water and bring to a boil over high heat. Reduce the heat to medium and cook for 20 minutes, or until fork-tender. Drain.

2. Meanwhile, make the Classic Oil and Vinegar Dressing In a small glass jar, combine the olive oil, parsley, garlic, red wine vinegar, mustard, and a pinch each of salt and pepper. Cover and shake well.

3. On a large platter, toss together the potatoes and black-eyed peas. Scatter the onion and olives on top. Arrange the Jammy Eggs on top and drizzle with the dressing. Season the eggs with salt and pepper and serve. Store any leftovers—without the eggs—in an airtight container in the fridge for up to 4 days.

Rainbow Chopped Salad

Serves 4 to 6 • **Prep Time 10 to 15 minutes**

Prep Ahead

Maple Tahini Dressing (page 230)

Ingredients

1 small yellow zucchini, cut into
    ½-inch cubes

1 small green zucchini, cut into
    ½-inch cubes

2 small carrots, peeled and
    cut into ½-inch cubes

2 cups chopped red cabbage

1 cup chopped broccoli florets

2 stalks celery, chopped

1 cup chopped strawberries

½ cup Maple Tahini Dressing

This is an adapted version of a salad my Tia Cris ("Aunt Cris" in Portuguese) makes all the time, and it's always a huge hit at barbecues and family gatherings. All the colours of the rainbow chopped into one crunchy, sweet, and savoury salad. There is just something so satisfying about a perfectly uniform chopped salad—it allows you to get all the different flavours and textures in every bite. So sharpen that knife and get chopping!

1. In a large salad bowl, combine the yellow zucchini, green zucchini, carrots, cabbage, broccoli, celery, and strawberries. Toss well.

2. Drizzle the Maple Tahini Dressing over the salad, toss again, and serve. Salad will keep in an airtight container in the fridge for up to 2 days with the dressing or up to 4 days without the dressing.

Nutty Noodle Summer Rolls

Makes 8 to 10 rolls • Prep Time 20 minutes • Cook Time 10 minutes

....

Marinated Tofu

1 block (14 ounces/398 g)
  extra-firm tofu

1 cup water

1 tablespoon unseasoned
  rice vinegar

1 tablespoon fresh lemon juice

1½ teaspoons gluten-free tamari

1 teaspoon toasted sesame oil

1 teaspoon sambal oelek
  (chili paste) or Sriracha

¼ teaspoon garlic powder

Sea salt and pepper

Almond Butter Sauce

(makes ¾ cup)

⅓ cup natural almond butter

¼ cup warm water

2 tablespoons gluten-free tamari

1 tablespoon sambal oelek
  (chili paste) or Sriracha

1 teaspoon toasted sesame oil

Juice of 1 lime

1 tablespoon pure maple syrup

Noodles

4 ounces (115 g) black rice
  noodles or soba noodles

1 tablespoon fresh lemon juice

1 teaspoon avocado oil

½ teaspoon toasted sesame oil

1 green onion (white and light
  green parts only), chopped

Sesame seeds

For Assembly

2 teaspoons avocado oil, for
  frying

8 to 10 rice-paper wrappers
  (8-inch wrappers)

1 small head butter lettuce

Small handful of fresh cilantro

1 cup peeled carrots cut into
  matchsticks

1 ripe avocado, pitted, peeled,
  and thinly sliced

½ cup chopped raw cashews

1 tablespoon sesame seeds

These colourful noodle summer rolls are filled with marinated fried tofu, a variety of crunchy veggies, and soft noodles, and served with a savoury almond butter sauce. Not only are rice-paper rolls fun to eat, but they are equally fun to make: once you have your ingredients prepped, you can show off your "sushi-making" skills and put together some fun creations. These fresh, flavourful rolls can be enjoyed on the go for lunch or cut up as appetizers.

HEALTHNUT TIP Unlike pasta, most Asian noodles (like soba) should be rinsed after cooking to prevent sticking and a gummy texture.

1. Prepare the Marinated Tofu Drain and pat dry the tofu, then cut it into small rectangles. In a deep bowl, combine the water, rice vinegar, lemon juice, tamari, sesame oil, sambal oelek, garlic powder, and a pinch each of salt and pepper; whisk together well. Submerge the tofu in the marinade, cover, and let marinate for 10 minutes.

2. Make the Almond Butter Sauce In a small blender, combine the almond butter, water, tamari, sambal oelek, sesame oil, lime juice, and maple syrup. Blend for 10 seconds, or until smooth. Set aside.

3. Prepare the Noodles Cook the noodles according to package directions. Drain, rinse with cold water, and transfer to a small bowl. Add the lemon juice, avocado oil, sesame oil, green onion, and a pinch of sesame seeds; toss well. Set aside.

recipe continues

4. **Fry the Tofu** Heat the avocado oil in a large skillet over medium heat. Drain the tofu and discard the marinade. Add the tofu to the skillet and cook for 5 to 8 minutes, or until brown on both sides, turning halfway through. Transfer to a plate and set aside to cool.

5. **Assemble the Summer Rolls** Pour hot water into a shallow dish. Working with one rice-paper wrapper at a time, immerse the wrapper in the water for 10 to 12 seconds to soften, flipping halfway through. Transfer to a cutting board or work surface slightly dampened with some water and gently spread out the edges so the wrapper lies flat. In the middle of the wrapper, arrange 1 or 2 lettuce leaves, a few sprigs of cilantro, 1 piece of tofu, some carrots, some noodles, and a slice of avocado. Sprinkle with some cashews and sesame seeds. Drizzle over some Almond Butter Sauce. Gently fold the bottom edge over the filling, fold in the sides, and continue rolling tightly. Repeat with the remaining rice-paper wrappers.

6. Serve with the remaining Almond Butter Sauce in a small bowl for dipping. Store any leftover rolls in an airtight container, separated by parchment paper, in the fridge for up to 3 days.

Grilled Vegetable Salad with Chimichurri

Serves 4 • **Prep Time 20 minutes** • **Cook Time 20 to 25 minutes**

Chimichurri

1 cup tightly packed fresh flat-leaf
   parsley
1 cup tightly packed fresh cilantro
3 cloves garlic, roughly chopped
⅓ cup extra-virgin olive oil
¼ cup red wine vinegar
Juice of ½ lemon
1 teaspoon dried oregano
1 teaspoon dried thyme
½ teaspoon red chili flakes
½ teaspoon sea salt
¼ teaspoon black pepper

Grilled Vegetable Salad

1 sweet red pepper
1 green zucchini, thinly sliced
   lengthwise on a mandoline
1 yellow zucchini, thinly sliced
   lengthwise on a mandoline
1 small red onion, thinly sliced
   into ½-inch wide strips
3 ounces (100 g) halloumi cheese,
   sliced ¼-inch thick
2 large heirloom tomatoes,
   cut into ½-inch wedges
Fresh cilantro, for garnish

This colourful summer-worthy grilled veggie salad, made with heirloom tomatoes, bell peppers, zucchini, and a herbed chimichurri sauce, is perfect for barbecue season. We'd always have a salad with our dinner when I was growing up, and since we're Portuguese and like to barbecue even in the middle of winter here in Canada, roasted peppers were something we enjoyed year round. Nowadays I "barbecue" in my condo using a grill pan on the stove and the broil setting on my oven. If you've never tried halloumi cheese before, it's a salty briny tasting cheese that has a meatier texture and stays firm when grilled. I like to call it the "bacon of cheeses," but either way you slice it, it's delicious.

1. **Make the Chimichurri** In a small food processor, combine the parsley, cilantro, garlic, olive oil, vinegar, lemon juice, oregano, thyme, chili flakes, salt, and black pepper. Process for 30 seconds. Set aside.

2. **Prepare the Grilled Vegetable Salad** Preheat the broiler. On a small baking sheet, broil the red pepper for 10 minutes on each side or until the skin is well blistered. Using tongs, transfer the pepper to an airtight container, cover, and set aside for 10 to 15 minutes for the skin to sweat off. Once cooled, peel off the skin, remove the stem and seeds, and slice the pepper into ¼-inch strips.

3. Heat a large grill pan (if you want grill marks) or skillet over medium-high heat. Dip the zucchini slices into the Chimichurri and grill the strips, turning once, until grill marks are visible or if using a skillet until golden and slightly crispy, 3 to 4 minutes each side. Transfer to a large bowl along with the cooked red pepper.

4. Reduce the heat to medium, dip the sliced onions and sliced halloumi into the Chimichurri, and cook, turning once, until grill marks are visible or if using a skillet until golden and slightly crispy, 2 to 3 minutes each side. Add the onions to the zucchini.

5. To the grilled vegetables, add the tomatoes and the remaining Chimichurri. Top with the grilled halloumi, cilantro and serve. Store any leftovers in an airtight container in the fridge for up to 2 days.

Shredded Caesar Salad

Serves 4 to 6 • **Prep Time 15 minutes**

....

Prep Ahead
Almond Flour Parm (page 225)

Ingredients
3 cups packed shredded Brussels
    sprouts (8 ounces/225 g)
2 cups stemmed and shredded
    black kale
1 cup shredded red cabbage
1 large ripe avocado, pitted, peeled,
    and diced
2 tablespoons Almond Flour Parm,
    for serving

Creamy Caesar Dressing
½ cup raw cashews (if not using a
    high-speed blender, soak in water
    for 4 to 6 hours or overnight)
1 clove garlic, chopped
Juice of ½ lemon
⅓ cup water
3 tablespoons extra-virgin olive oil
2 teaspoons caper brine
1 tablespoon nutritional yeast
1 teaspoon gluten-free tamari
Sea salt and pepper
2 teaspoons capers, minced

The Caesar is that classic favourite salad that you order at restaurants to make you feel good about eating greens, but usually it contains more cheese and oil than actual lettuce. My version is a purple and green salad with the most creamy dressing, delicious as a side at dinner or as a complete meal with grilled salmon or a poached egg on top. This shredded Caesar is not only one you can feel good about eating, but also hearty, flavourful—and dairy-free!

1. In a large salad bowl, toss together the Brussels sprouts, kale, and red cabbage.

2. **Make the Creamy Caesar Dressing** In a high-speed blender, combine the cashews, garlic, lemon juice, water, olive oil, caper brine, nutritional yeast, tamari, and a pinch each of salt and pepper. Blend until smooth and creamy, about 40 seconds. Stir in the minced capers.

3. Drizzle the Creamy Caesar Dressing over the salad and toss until well coated. Scatter the avocado on top, sprinkle with Almond Flour Parm, and serve. Salad will keep in an airtight container in the fridge for up to 2 days with the dressing or up to 4 days without the dressing.

VARIATION Enjoy with a side of grilled chicken, crispy tofu, or pan-seared salmon.

HEALTHNUT TIP I like to use the slicing disc attachment of my food processor to shred the Brussels sprouts, kale, and cabbage. I recommend making the dressing the day before so the garlic and cheesy flavours can really pop through.

Greek Chicken Salad with Spiced Chickpeas

Serves 4 • **Prep Time 15 minutes** • **Cook Time 25 minutes**

Zesty Greek Dressing

¼ cup extra-virgin olive oil

¼ cup loosely packed fresh flat-leaf
parsley, finely chopped

1 clove garlic, finely chopped

Juice of ½ lemon

1 tablespoon red wine vinegar

1 teaspoon pure liquid honey

½ teaspoon za'atar

½ teaspoon sumac

¼ teaspoon sea salt

Pepper

Spiced Chickpeas

1 can (14 ounces/398 mL)
chickpeas, rinsed and drained
(or 1½ cups cooked chickpeas)

1 tablespoon avocado oil

1 teaspoon za'atar

1 teaspoon sumac

¼ teaspoon sea salt

Pepper

Greek Chicken Salad

1 tablespoon fresh lemon juice

3 teaspoons extra-virgin olive oil,
divided

½ teaspoon za'atar

¼ teaspoon sea salt

Pepper

2 boneless, skinless chicken breasts
(8 ounces/225 g each)

1 head romaine lettuce, chopped
(3 cups packed)

1 cup chopped cucumber

1 cup cherry tomatoes, halved

½ cup chopped red onion

¼ cup pitted Kalamata olives

¼ cup crumbled feta cheese

Whether it's salad, chicken, or weddings, the Greeks just seem to know what they're doing. I've always been a huge fan of anything Mediterranean when it comes to food. They have some of the best fresh and zesty flavours that can be enjoyed either raw in salads or cooked with meat, fish, and veggies. I opted for Middle Eastern spices like za'atar and sumac for a unique, aromatic, and tangy kick that complements this dish so well. In this salad, the combination of colours and textures from the acidic tomatoes mixed with crunchy cucumber, spicy red onion, salty feta, and olives just makes me want to break a plate and yell "Opa!"

1. **Make the Zesty Greek Dressing** In a small bowl, combine the olive oil, parsley, garlic, lemon juice, red wine vinegar, honey, za'atar, sumac, salt, and a pinch of pepper. Whisk until emulsified. Set aside.

2. **Make the Spiced Chickpeas** Preheat the oven to 400°F. Line a baking sheet with parchment paper. In a medium bowl, combine the chickpeas, avocado oil, za'atar, sumac, salt, and a pinch of pepper. Toss to coat. Spread on the prepared baking sheet and bake for 25 minutes, or until golden and crispy, stirring halfway through. Set aside.

3. **Make the Greek Chicken Salad** In a medium bowl, stir together the lemon juice, 1½ teaspoons of the olive oil, za'atar, salt, and a pinch of pepper. Add the chicken and turn to coat.

4. Heat the remaining 1½ teaspoons olive oil in a large skillet over medium-high heat. Add the chicken and cook for 10 minutes, or until the edges are opaque. Turn, cover, reduce the heat to medium, and cook for another 10 minutes, or until cooked through. Transfer the chicken to a cutting board and let rest for 5 minutes before cutting into ½-inch slices.

5. To assemble the salad, in a large bowl, combine the lettuce, cucumber, tomatoes, onion, and olives. Drizzle the dressing over the salad and toss to coat.

6. Layer the sliced chicken breasts on top, sprinkle with Roasted Chickpeas and feta cheese, and serve. Salad will keep in an airtight container in the fridge for 1 day with the dressing or up to 2 days without the dressing.

VARIATION You can replace za'atar and sumac with equal amounts of Italian seasoning and paprika.

Beauty Glow Salad

Serves 4 • **Prep Time 15 minutes**

Creamy Lemon Ginger Dressing

¼ cup tahini

½ cup water

Juice of ½ lemon

2 tablespoons extra-virgin olive oil

1 tablespoon pure liquid honey

1 tablespoon apple cider vinegar

½-inch piece peeled fresh ginger, minced

½-inch piece peeled fresh turmeric, minced (or ½ teaspoon ground turmeric)

Beauty Glow Salad

4 cups tightly packed stemmed and chopped curly kale (mix of purple and green)

1 tablespoon fresh lemon juice

1 tablespoon extra-virgin olive oil

Sea salt

1 head butter lettuce, torn

1 large sweet red pepper, thinly sliced

1 English cucumber, thinly sliced

6 small radishes, thinly sliced

1 green onion (white and light green parts only), thinly sliced

¼ cup thinly sliced red onion

¼ cup chopped fresh cilantro

¼ cup raw pumpkin seeds

1 ripe avocado, pitted, peeled, and sliced

½ cup pomegranate seeds, for garnish

This hydrating vitamin-infused salad is what I call real, organic, non-toxic skincare for your skin. Rich in antioxidants from the deep colours and healthy fats in the avocado and seeds, this salad will make your skin glow from within. The perfect mix of crunchy, fresh, and buttery with a creamy lemon ginger dressing makes this a great light lunch or side salad. I like to make this salad when I feel like I've been eating a little too much processed food and my body just needs a little pick-me-up. Trust me, your skin will thank you.

1. **Make the Creamy Lemon Ginger Dressing** In a high-speed blender, combine the tahini, water, lemon juice, olive oil, honey, cider vinegar, ginger, and turmeric. Blend on high speed until smooth, 30 to 40 seconds.

2. **Make the Beauty Glow Salad** In a large bowl, combine the kale, lemon juice, olive oil, and a pinch of salt. Massage the kale with your hands for 30 to 60 seconds to soften. Add the lettuce, red pepper, cucumber, radishes, green onion, red onion, cilantro, and pumpkin seeds; toss to combine.

3. Drizzle the salad with the desired amount of Creamy Lemon Ginger Dressing and toss to coat. Top with avocado slices and sprinkle with pomegranate seeds. Serve immediately. Store any leftover dressing in a glass jar in the fridge for up to 5 days.

🌰 **HEALTHNUT TIP** If the dressing is too thick, thin it out by blending in 1 tablespoon of water at a time.

Apple Bacon Kale Salad

Serves 4 to 6 • **Prep Time 10 minutes**

Prep Ahead

Crispy Oven Bacon (page 222)

Maple Tahini Dressing (page 230)

Ingredients

4 cups tightly packed stemmed and
    shredded curly kale

1 ripe avocado, pitted, peeled, and
    cut into ½-inch cubes

1 apple (Pink Lady or Fuji), cored
    and cut into ½-inch cubes

½ cup fresh blueberries

¼ cup dried cranberries

¼ cup raw pecan halves

¼ cup raw sunflower seeds

6 strips Crispy Oven Bacon,
    cooled and roughly chopped

½ cup Maple Tahini Dressing

If you've been hunting for the ultimate loaded kale salad with everything from apple to bacon, smothered in the most delicious maple tahini dressing, look no further. You might be thinking, "Bacon and kale—isn't that an oxymoron or something?" Well, they say opposites attract, and in this case it couldn't be more true. My younger sister has made this so many times that everyone in the family calls it Cloe's salad. Since little sisters steal everything, I guess I'll just let her take this too. I'm just happy everyone's getting some greens into their day.

1. In a large salad bowl, combine the kale, avocado, apple, blueberries, cranberries, pecans, sunflower seeds, and bacon.

2. Drizzle the Maple Tahini Dressing over the salad, toss to coat, and serve. Store any leftovers in an airtight container in the fridge for up to 2 days.

🌰 **HEALTHNUT TIP** Because kale is a heartier green, you can store it in an airtight container in the fridge for up to 2 days with the dressing mixed in and it will not go soggy.

Where's Waldorf? Salad

Serves 4 to 6 • Prep Time 10 minutes • Cook Time 5 minutes

Creamy Dijon Yogurt Dressing

¼ cup plain full-fat yogurt or
    coconut yogurt

2 tablespoons extra-virgin olive oil

1 tablespoon apple cider vinegar

1 tablespoon water

2 teaspoons grainy Dijon mustard

1½ teaspoons pure liquid honey

Sea salt and pepper

Where's Waldorf? Salad

½ cup roughly chopped raw
    walnuts

1 head butter lettuce, roughly torn

3 stalks celery, sliced

1 apple (Pink Lady or Fuji), cored
    and thinly sliced

1 cup red grapes, halved

This salad was on my to-make list for quite some time, and let me tell you, it was worth the wait! It's light and fresh, with the perfect combination of sweetness and crunch. Everyday staples like apples, celery, walnuts, and lettuce for a variety of textures and flavours. The classic Waldorf recipe has a mayonnaise-based dressing, but I've swapped that out for a light tangy yogurt and Dijon mustard dressing that ties everything together. Enjoy this salad as a light lunch or on a hot summer day at a family barbecue on the deck. There is really no wrong way to eat this updated Waldorf salad.

1. **Make the Creamy Dijon Yogurt Dressing** In a small glass jar, combine the yogurt, olive oil, cider vinegar, water, mustard, honey, and a pinch each of salt and pepper. Cover and shake well. Store the dressing in the jar in the fridge for up to 2 days.

2. **Make the Where's Waldorf? Salad** In a medium skillet over medium-high heat, toast the walnuts for 4 to 5 minutes, stirring frequently. Set aside to cool slightly.

3. In a large salad bowl, combine the lettuce, celery, apple, grapes, and walnuts. Drizzle the Creamy Dijon Yogurt Dressing on top, toss to coat, and serve immediately. Salad will keep, without the dressing, in an airtight container in the fridge for up to 2 days.

Lemon Dill Mashed Bean "Egg" Salad

Serves 4 • **Prep Time 10 minutes**

Ingredients

1 cup canned chickpeas, rinsed
and drained (or 1 cup cooked
chickpeas)

1 cup canned cannellini beans,
rinsed and drained (or 1 cup
cooked cannellini beans)

1 green onion (white and light
green parts only), sliced

Juice of ½ lemon

¼ cup vegan or regular mayonnaise

1 tablespoon drained capers

1 teaspoon chopped fresh dill

½ teaspoon ground turrmeric

½ teaspoon sea salt

¼ teaspoon pepper

¼ teaspoon sweet paprika

When I'm craving egg salad, I'll whip up this classic-with-a-twist for a delicious lunch. Packed with protein and fibre, and made with pantry staples, this vegan egg salad will become your go-to brown bag favourite without offending any noses in the lunchroom! Slather it between two slices of dark rye and top with lettuce, tomato, dill pickles, and alfalfa sprouts for a smell-free egg salad sandwich that you'll want to savour again and again.

1. In a food processor, combine the chickpeas, cannellini beans, green onion, lemon juice, mayonnaise, capers, dill, turmeric, salt, pepper, and paprika. Pulse for about 15 seconds, until smooth with a bit of texture. Store in an airtight container in the fridge for up to 5 days.

🌰 **HEALTHNUT TIP** Try not to overprocess the beans or you will end up with hummus instead of an egg salad copycat!

Watermelon Cucumber Quinoa Salad

Serves 4 to 6 • Prep Time 12 minutes

Prep Ahead
Fluffy Cooked Quinoa (page 219)

Ingredients
1½ cups Fluffy Cooked Quinoa
1 English cucumber, chopped
2 cups cubed watermelon
½ cup thinly sliced red onion
½ cup crumbled goat feta cheese

Basil and Mint Vinaigrette
½ cup extra-virgin olive oil
¼ cup white wine vinegar
Juice of ½ lemon
1 tablespoon pure liquid honey
¼ cup finely chopped fresh basil
¼ cup finely chopped fresh mint
Sea salt and pepper

Basically summer in a bowl, this salad screams barbecues, pool parties, and picnics in the park. Made with five simple ingredients—juicy watermelon, crisp cucumber, shaved red onion, crumbled feta, and fluffy quinoa—it's easy to prep the day before and pack with you wherever you go to catch some sunshine. Oh, and can we just talk about this dressing for a second? The summery, fresh basil and mint combo goes perfectly with this salad for a burst of freshness in every bite.

1. In a large salad bowl, combine the cooked quinoa, cucumber, watermelon, onion, and feta. Toss well.

2. **Make the Basil and Mint Vinaigrette** In a small glass jar, combine the olive oil, white wine vinegar, lemon juice, honey, basil, mint, and a pinch each of salt and pepper. Cover and shake well.

3. Drizzle the salad with the desired amount of Basil and Mint Vinaigrette, toss to coat, and serve. Store any leftovers in an airtight container in the fridge for up to 2 days.

🌰 **HEALTHNUT TIP** On the go? Pack this salad into a couple of tall wide-mouth jars, starting with the dressing at the bottom, followed by the quinoa, cucumber, onion, watermelon, and feta. Follow the rule of heaviest to lightest and you can use this method with most of your favourite salads.

PLATES

and

BOWLS

Mushrooms on Toast

Serves 1 or 2 • **Prep Time 3 minutes** • **Cook Time 9 to 11 minutes**

Prep Ahead

Lemon Herb White Bean Hummus
  (page 79)

Ingredients

1½ teaspoons extra-virgin olive oil

1 clove garlic, minced

2 cups sliced mushrooms
  (I like shimeji)

2 sprigs fresh thyme, leaves stripped
  from the stems, divided

Sea salt and pepper

2 slices sourdough or gluten-free
  bread

½ cup Lemon Herb White Bean
  Hummus

Everything tastes better when served on a slice of toast, am I right? Especially when it's a slice of your favourite rustic sourdough bread covered in sautéed mushrooms. This savoury, buttery, textured toastie is delish with the sautéed thyme mushrooms and creamy white bean hummus. Enjoy on its own as a snack, as a side with a bowl of hot chili or soup, or paired with a fried egg. Move aside, avocado toast, because this one is going to be a trendsetter!

1. Heat the olive oil in a medium skillet over medium heat. Add the garlic and cook for 1 minute, stirring frequently. Add the mushrooms, half of the thyme, and a pinch each of salt and pepper. Cook, stirring frequently, until the mushrooms are tender and slightly golden brown at the edges, 8 to 10 minutes.

2. To assemble, toast the bread. Spread a thick layer of Lemon Herb White Bean Hummus on top. Top with the sautéed mushrooms, garnish with the remaining thyme, and serve.

VARIATION   Feel free to play around with other veggies, such as zucchini, radishes, or leafy greens like spinach or kale.

Rad Avocado Toast

Serves 1 or 2 • **Prep Time 10 minutes**

Ingredients

2 radishes, thinly sliced

Sea salt

1 large ripe avocado, pitted,
  and peeled

Zest of ½ lemon

1 tablespoon fresh lemon juice

2 teaspoons thinly sliced fresh mint

Garlic powder

Pepper

2 slices sourdough or gluten-free
  bread

¼ cup spring pea microgreen mix

By now, many of us have experienced the magic that is avocado toast. Let's just say this version is the cool uncle. Buttery mashed avocado with the zing of lemon and mint for a refreshing twist on the popular dish that is far from basic. If you're going to have some avocado toast, you might as well make it rad!

1. In a small bowl, combine the sliced radishes and a pinch of salt. Stir well, then set aside for 5 minutes.

2. In a separate small bowl, combine the avocado, lemon zest, lemon juice, mint, and a pinch each of salt, garlic powder, and pepper. Mash with a fork, leaving the avocado chunky.

3. To assemble, toast the bread. Smear the toast with the avocado mash, then top with a layer of sliced radishes. Season with a pinch each of salt and pepper, top with microgreens, and serve.

VARIATION For a quick lunch or light dinner, top with a poached egg or some canned tuna.

Southwest Black-Eyed Pea Burgers

Makes 4 burgers • Prep Time 10 minutes • Cook Time 15 minutes

Prep Ahead

Avocado Ranch Dip (page 229)

Caramelized Veggies

1 tablespoon extra-virgin olive oil

1 sweet red pepper, thinly sliced

½ red onion, thinly sliced

Smoked paprika

Sea salt and pepper

Southwest Black-Eyed Pea Burgers

1 can (14 ounces/398 mL) black-eyed peas, rinsed and drained (or 1½ cups cooked black-eyed peas)

½ sweet red pepper, chopped

2 cremini mushrooms, stemmed and chopped

2 cloves garlic, minced

½ cayenne chili pepper, seeded and finely chopped

½ cup corn kernels, thawed if frozen

¼ cup finely chopped red onion

¼ cup loosely packed chopped fresh flat-leaf parsley

2 tablespoons plain full-fat yogurt or coconut yogurt

1 egg

Juice of 1 lime

½ teaspoon ground cumin

½ teaspoon smoked sweet paprika

½ teaspoon chipotle chili powder

½ teaspoon sea salt

¼ teaspoon black pepper

½ cup gluten-free rice bread crumbs

2 tablespoons avocado oil, for frying

4 whole grain or gluten-free hamburger buns

Garnishes

Butter lettuce

Sliced tomato

1 batch Avocado Ranch Dip

I've had my fair share of bean patties in my lifetime, but using the underrated black-eyed pea for the base of this Southwest-inspired burger is a huge game changer! So if you're a vegetarian, or looking for a new meatless protein-packed meal for your family, this is a must-try! I'm a firm believer that a burger is only as good as its toppings, so I did not go light in that regard. Caramelized onions and sweet peppers, crisp lettuce, juicy tomato, and my Avocado Ranch Dip (page 229) round out this "meat-eater-approved" veggie burger.

1. **Make the Caramelized Veggies** Heat the olive oil in a medium skillet over medium heat. Add the red peppers, onions, and a pinch each of paprika, salt, and pepper. Cook, stirring frequently, for 10 minutes, or until the peppers are soft and the onions are translucent and caramelized.

2. **Make the Southwest Black-Eyed Pea Burgers** In a food processor, combine the black-eyed peas, red pepper, mushrooms, garlic, chili pepper, corn, onion, parsley, yogurt, egg, lime juice, cumin, paprika, chipotle powder, salt, and black pepper; process for 10 to 15 seconds until the mixture sticks together with some texture. You are not going for a purée. Transfer the mixture to a large bowl and stir in the bread crumbs.

3. Divide the burger mixture into 4 equal portions and shape into about ½-inch-thick patties.

4. In a large skillet, heat the avocado oil over medium-high heat. Working in batches, fry the patties for 3 to 4 minutes on each side until browned and heated through. Transfer to a plate and repeat until all the patties are cooked.

5. Place each burger on the bottom half of a bun and garnish with warm Caramelized Veggies, lettuce, tomato, and Avocado Ranch Dip. Store any leftover burgers in an airtight container in the fridge for up to 5 days or cool, transfer to a resealable freezer bag, and freeze for up to 1 month.

VARIATION Instead of frying the burgers, arrange on a lightly oiled baking sheet and bake at 400°F for 20 minutes, flipping halfway through.

HEALTHNUT TIP Skip the bun and have a naked-style burger. Wrap it in lettuce for a refreshing gluten-free crunch.

Salmon Burgers with Pineapple Salsa

Makes 6 burgers • Prep Time 15 minutes • Cook Time 15 to 18 minutes

Pineapple Salsa

2 cups finely diced fresh pineapple

1 cup finely diced sweet red pepper

1 cup finely diced tomato

¼ cup loosely packed fresh cilantro,
   chopped

¼ red onion, finely chopped

1 small jalapeño pepper, seeded
   and finely diced

Juice of 1 lime

Sea salt and pepper

Salmon Burgers

12 ounces (340 g) skinless
   wild salmon fillet

¼ teaspoon sea salt, divided

2 eggs, lightly beaten

1 small shallot, finely chopped

2 cloves garlic, minced

5 fresh basil leaves

Juice of ½ lemon

1 teaspoon grainy Dijon mustard

½ cup gluten-free rice bread crumbs

¼ teaspoon smoked sweet paprika

¼ teaspoon garlic powder

¼ teaspoon pepper

1 to 2 tablespoons avocado oil,
   for frying

1 small head butter lettuce
   (optional)

6 whole grain burger buns
   (optional)

1 ripe avocado, pitted, peeled,
   and sliced

When the hot weather hits, all I crave is grilled salmon, so naturally I turned it into burgers. Simple ingredients like fresh basil, garlic, shallot, and lemon combine to make a drool-worthy summer burger you'll want to sink your teeth into. Serve it "naked," on lettuce with avocado and a side of my sweet and spicy pineapple salsa, and you have yourself a perfect lunch or dinner.

1. **Make the Pineapple Salsa** In a large bowl, combine the pineapple, red pepper, tomato, cilantro, red onion, jalapeño, lime juice, and a pinch each of salt and pepper. Give it a good stir to mix all the flavours together. Cover and refrigerate to let the flavours mingle while you make the salmon burgers.

2. **Make the Salmon Burgers** Put the salmon in a shallow pot, add water to come three-quarters of the way up the side of the fish, and add a pinch of salt. Bring to a boil, then reduce the heat to medium and cook for 7 to 10 minutes until opaque and the fish flakes easily with a fork. Poaching time may vary depending on the thickness of your fish. Transfer the salmon to a large bowl and shred it with a fork. Add the lightly beaten eggs, shallot, garlic, basil, lemon juice, mustard, bread crumbs, paprika, garlic powder, the remaining salt, and pepper. Mix with a wooden spoon or rubber spatula until well combined.

3. Divide the burger mixture into 6 equal portions and shape into ½-inch-thick patties. Place the patties on a parchment-lined baking sheet or plate.

4. Heat the avocado oil in a large non-stick skillet over medium heat (or prepare a grill for direct cooking over medium heat). Place the patties in the hot pan (or on the grill) and cook for 3 to 4 minutes, until golden brown on the bottom. Flip the burgers and cook for another 3 to 4 minutes, until golden brown.

5. Serve in a butter lettuce wrap (or on a bun with the lettuce inside) and top with avocado slices and Pineapple Salsa. Store any leftover cooled cooked salmon burgers in an airtight container in the fridge for up to 3 days or transfer to a resealable freezer bag and freeze for up to 1 month.

VARIATION In a pinch you can use 2 cans (6 ounces/170 g each) of boneless, skinless wild salmon in place of poached salmon.

🐿 **HEALTHNUT TIP** You can prepare the salmon mixture the night before, store in an airtight container in the fridge, and cook the next day.

Falafel Mediterranean Bowl

Makes 12 falafel balls; serves 4 • Prep Time 15 minutes • Cook Time 15 minutes

....

Prep Ahead

Beet Goat Cheese Hummus
(page 80)
Maple Tahini Dressing (page 230)
Fluffy Cooked Quinoa (page 219)

Falafel Balls

1 cup dried chickpeas, soaked
in water for 24 hours and
drained (see Tip)
¾ cup roughly chopped
yellow onion
4 cloves garlic, roughly
chopped
½ cup finely chopped
fresh flat-leaf parsley
½ cup finely chopped
fresh cilantro
¼ cup oat flour
1 teaspoon sea salt
1 teaspoon baking powder
1 teaspoon ground cumin
1 teaspoon ground coriander
¼ teaspoon smoked sweet
paprika
¼ teaspoon pepper
2 eggs
2 to 3 tablespoons avocado oil,
for frying

Quinoa Tabbouleh Salad

2 cups Fluffy Cooked Quinoa
1 bunch fresh curly parsley,
chopped
½ English cucumber, diced
1 clove garlic, minced
1 cup cherry tomatoes,
quartered
½ cup chopped red onion
2 tablespoons chopped
fresh mint
¼ teaspoon ground cumin
¼ teaspoon sea salt
¼ teaspoon pepper
¼ cup extra-virgin olive oil
Juice of 1½ lemons

Toppings

½ cup Beet Goat Cheese
Hummus
Peperoncini peppers (optional)
Kalamata olives (optional)
Chopped raw pistachios
(optional)
1 batch Maple Tahini Dressing

Crispy on the outside, soft and tender on the inside, these savoury, spice-packed little Mediterranean gems are a vegetarian's dream. You've probably had falafels from one of those corner shawarma spots, but I'm telling you, nothing compares to the fresh homemade stuff warm from the pan. These are packed with fibre and protein from the chickpeas, making them a perfect filling meal for meatless Monday or a delicious snack to have with hummus when you get home after a long day. I like my falafel extra herby, with lots of spices, and pan-fried for that perfect crispy outside.

🍲 **HEALTHNUT TIP** For a quick hack, you can use 3 cans (14 ounces/398 mL each) chickpeas, rinsed and drained, instead of dried and soaked chickpeas. The texture will be softer but still yummy. First process all of the ingredients except the chickpeas, then add the chickpeas and pulse for only a few seconds—just enough to combine. Otherwise you might end up with hummus!

1. **Make the Falafel Balls** In a food processor, combine the chickpeas, onions, garlic, parsley, cilantro, oat flour, salt, baking powder, cumin, coriander, paprika, pepper, and eggs. Process for 5 minutes, stopping to scrape down the sides when needed. Using your hands, roll about 3 tablespoons of falafel mixture at a time into twelve ½-inch small pucks.

2. Heat the avocado oil in a large skillet over medium heat. Working in batches if necessary, fry the pucks for 2 to 3 minutes on each side, until golden brown and heated through. Transfer to a plate lined with paper towel.

3. **Make the Quinoa Tabbouleh Salad** In a large bowl, combine the Fluffy Cooked Quinoa, parsley, cucumber, garlic, tomatoes, red onion, mint, cumin, salt, pepper, olive oil, and lemon juice. Toss to combine.

4. To assemble, divide the Quinoa Tabbouleh Salad among 4 bowls. Top each bowl with 3 Falafel Balls, 2 tablespoons Beet Goat Cheese Hummus, and any optional toppings. Drizzle with Maple Tahini Dressing and serve. Store leftovers in separate airtight containers in the fridge for up to 3 days.

Farmers' Market Bowl

Serves 2 • Prep Time 10 to 15 minutes • Cook Time 20 to 25 minutes

Prep Ahead

Fluffy Cooked Quinoa (page 219)

Ingredients

1 cup French green beans cut into
   1-inch pieces

½ cup fresh or frozen peas

½ cup fresh or frozen corn kernels

1 teaspoon extra-virgin olive oil,
   divided

1 boneless, skinless chicken breast
   (8 ounces/225 g)

3½ ounces (100 g) halloumi cheese

2 cups tightly packed stemmed and
   chopped kale

1 cup Fluffy Cooked Quinoa

1 cup halved cherry tomatoes

½ cup pitted Kalamata olives

Lemon Vinaigrette Dressing

¼ cup extra-virgin olive oil

Zest of ½ lemon

1 tablespoon fresh lemon juice

1 tablespoon apple cider vinegar

1½ teaspoons pure liquid honey

1 teaspoon Dijon mustard

Sea salt and pepper

Who doesn't love going to the farmers' market? I like to arrive hungry and taste-test all the seasonal offerings while getting some vitamin D and friendly conversation. Knowing where my food comes from is important to me, and changing up my menu with what's in season and local means my meals taste better and are more budget friendly! Although I'm a huge advocate of making a grocery list, I sometimes love to go with no agenda and just buy what speaks to me. This recipe was inspired by produce that I love to get from my local farmers' market: corn, peas, tomatoes, kale, and cheese. Grab your tote bag, get exploring, and maybe try that odd-looking root vegetable with the name you can hardly pronounce.

1. In a medium saucepan of salted boiling water, blanch the green beans, fresh or frozen peas, and frozen corn for 4 minutes. If using fresh corn, remove the kernels from the cob with a sharp knife. In a separate saucepan of salted boiling water, boil the fresh corn for 10 minutes until soft and bright yellow. Drain and rinse all the veggies under cold water, then drain again.

2. Heat a medium grill pan or skillet over medium-high heat. Brush the pan with some of the olive oil. Add the chicken and cook for 10 minutes, or until the edges are opaque. Turn, cover, reduce the heat to medium-low, and cook for another 10 minutes, or until cooked through. Transfer the chicken to a cutting board and let rest for 5 minutes before cutting into ½-inch slices.

3. Meanwhile, make the Lemon Vinaigrette Dressing In a small glass jar, combine the olive oil, lemon zest, lemon juice, cider vinegar, honey, mustard, and a pinch each of salt and pepper. Cover and shake until emulsified.

4. Wipe the pan clean and return to medium heat. Cut the halloumi into ¼-inch slices, pat dry, and brush with some of the olive oil. Cook for 1 to 2 minutes on each side, until golden.

5. In a large bowl, toss the kale with the Fluffy Cooked Quinoa. Divide between 2 large bowls. Spoon the green beans, peas, corn, tomatoes, and olives on top. Arrange the sliced grilled chicken and the halloumi on top, drizzle with the Lemon Vinaigrette Dressing, and serve. Store any leftovers in an airtight container in the fridge for up to 3 days.

Roasted Acorn Squash Nourish Bowl

Serves 4 • Prep Time 10 minutes • Bake Time 25 to 30 minutes

Prep Ahead

Fluffy Cooked Quinoa (page 219)
Maple Tahini Dressing (page 230)

Ingredients

1 small acorn squash
2 tablespoons avocado oil, divided
Sea salt and pepper
1 red onion, quartered
1 can (14 ounces/398 mL)
  chickpeas, rinsed and drained
  (or 1½ cups cooked chickpeas)
¼ teaspoon sweet paprika
4 cups tightly packed stemmed
  and chopped kale
1 tablespoon extra-virgin olive oil
1 tablespoon fresh lemon juice
Sea salt and pepper
3 cups Fluffy Cooked Quinoa

Toppings

1 large ripe avocado, pitted,
  peeled, and sliced
2 cups alfalfa sprouts
¼ cup pomegranate seeds
1 batch Maple Tahini Dressing

I discovered acorn squash in college, when I received one in a monthly food delivery box I had signed up for. After it sat on my kitchen counter for weeks, I decided to throw it into the oven and roast it. The buttery roasted flavour swept me off my feet, and I've been on the squash and pumpkin bandwagon ever since. This nourishing bowl not only is beautiful but also encompasses autumn with all the colours and seasonal produce. There is just something about a variety of flavours all mingled together into one bowl, with a bomb sauce, that makes me feel all cozy inside.

1. Position the oven racks in the upper and lower thirds of the oven and preheat the oven to 400°F. Line 2 baking sheets with parchment paper.

2. Cut off the ends of the squash. Halve the squash and scoop out and discard the seeds. Slice the squash crosswise into ¼-inch-thick crescents. Arrange the slices in a single layer on one of the prepared baking sheets. Drizzle with 1 tablespoon of the avocado oil, sprinkle with a pinch each of salt and pepper, and massage the oil and seasonings over the squash.

3. On the second prepared baking sheet, place the onion and chickpeas and drizzle with the remaining 1 tablespoon avocado oil and sprinkle with paprika and a pinch each of salt and pepper. Massage the oil and seasonings over the onion wedges and chickpeas. Slide both baking sheets in the oven and roast, for 15 minutes. Turn the squash and stir the onion and chickpeas, switching sheets on racks, and roast for another 10 to 15 minutes or until golden brown and fork-tender.

4. Meanwhile in a large bowl, combine the kale, olive oil, lemon juice, and a pinch of salt. Massage the kale with your hands for 30 seconds to soften.

5. To assemble, divide the Fluffy Cooked Quinoa among 4 bowls (about ¾ cup per bowl). Top with squash slices, kale, and the onion and chickpea mixture. Top with avocado slices, alfalfa sprouts, and a sprinkle of pomegranate seeds. Drizzle with Maple Tahini Dressing and serve. Store any leftovers in an airtight container, without toppings, for up to 3 days.

HEALTHNUT TIP Did you know most squash and pumpkin skins are edible? Yes! Skip the peeling and leave it on and roast until nice and crispy in the oven.

Mushroom Fettuccine Alfredo

Serves 6 • **Soak Time 4 to 6 hours or overnight** • **Prep Time 10 minutes** • **Cook Time 20 minutes**

Prep Ahead
Almond Flour Parm (page 225)

Cashew Cream
½ cup raw cashews
½ cup water
1 tablespoon fresh lemon juice

Mushroom Fettuccine
14 ounces (400 g) brown rice
  fettuccine
2 tablespoons extra-virgin olive oil
2 cups thinly sliced king oyster
  mushrooms
1 small shallot, finely chopped
3 cloves garlic, minced
½ vegetable bouillon cube
3 sprigs fresh thyme, leaves stripped
  from the stems
2 tablespoons finely chopped
  fresh basil
½ teaspoon sweet paprika
½ teaspoon sea salt
¼ teaspoon pepper,
  more for garnish

Garnishes
2 tablespoons chopped fresh
  flat-leaf parsley
¼ cup Almond Flour Parm

When I was growing up, fettuccine Alfredo was my go-to order at restaurants. What's not to love? It's a dreamy, creamy, garlicky, cheesy plate of white pasta. Problem is, I would always leave the restaurant feeling bloated from all that cream. This "no to dairy but yes to flavour" Alfredo dish was one of the first recipes I ever made when I discovered the wonders of cashew cream. I'm telling you, it's magic! It will fool the pickiest of pasta eaters, and they'll be coming back for seconds and thirds—so be sure to make extra.

1. **Make the Cashew Cream** Soak the cashews in enough water to cover for 4 to 6 hours or overnight.

2. Drain and rinse the cashews and transfer them to a high-speed blender. Add the water and lemon juice and blend until smooth. Set aside.

3. **Make the Mushroom Fettuccine** Bring a large pot of salted water to a boil and cook the fettuccine until just tender, 9 to 11 minutes or according to package directions. Reserve 1 cup of the pasta water for the sauce, then drain the pasta and rinse well with cold water. I know it sounds wrong, but this stops the cooking and prevents the noodles from sticking together. Set aside.

4. In a large saucepan, heat the olive oil over medium heat. Add the mushrooms and shallots and cook for 2 to 3 minutes until slightly golden and fragrant, stirring occasionally. Add the garlic and cook for 1 minute. Pour in the reserved pasta water and give it a good stir.

5. Add the bouillon cube, thyme, basil, paprika, salt, and pepper. Simmer for 3 minutes, stirring occasionally.

6. Reduce the heat to low and stir in the Cashew Cream. Cover and cook for another 2 minutes, or until the sauce starts to thicken.

7. Remove from the heat and stir in the cooked pasta. Allow the sauce to warm up the pasta before serving. Divide among shallow bowls, garnish with parsley, pepper, and a sprinkle of Almond Flour Parm, and serve. This pasta is best enjoyed the same day, but leftovers can be stored in an airtight container in the fridge for up to 3 days. When reheating add a bit of water to help loosen up the sauce again.

VARIATION Add sliced cooked chicken breast or tiger shrimp for an extra protein kick.

Easy Peasy Pesto Pasta

Serves 4 • Prep Time 5 minutes • Cook Time 10 to 12 minutes

Prep Ahead
Easy Peasy Pesto (page 227)
Almond Flour Parm (page 225)

Ingredients
3 cups brown rice mini pasta shells
½ cup Easy Peasy Pesto
½ cup fresh or thawed frozen
 green peas
¼ cup sliced sun-dried tomatoes
¼ cup Almond Flour Parm
Fresh basil and mint leaves,
 for garnish

Brown rice pasta shells covered in a garlicky, lemony basil pesto with an unexpected hit of mint that gives this dish a summer-fresh flavour—even if you're eating it in the dead of winter. Tangy sun-dried tomatoes add a pop of colour to this delicious, easy pasta.

1. Cook the pasta in a large pot of boiling salted water until just tender, 10 to 12 minutes, stirring occasionally. Drain and rinse the pasta. Drain well again and transfer to a large bowl.

2. Add the Easy Peasy Pesto and stir until well coated. Stir in the peas, tomatoes, and a generous sprinkle of Almond Flour Parm. Serve warm or cold, garnished with fresh basil and mint. Store any leftovers in an airtight container in the fridge for up to 4 days.

VARIATION Add sautéed shrimp or grilled chicken for a protein boost.

HEALTHNUT TIP If you're eating leftovers or using it in your weekly meal prep, enjoy as a cold pasta salad.

Baked Mac and Cheese, Please

Serves 4 to 6 • **Prep Time 15 minutes** • **Bake Time 35 to 40 minutes**

Prep Ahead

Nacho Average Cheese Sauce
  (page 226)
Fluffy Cooked Quinoa (page 219)
Almond Flour Parm (page 225)

Ingredients

12 ounces (340 g) brown rice
  elbow macaroni
1 batch Nacho Average Cheese
  Sauce, warmed
½ cup gluten-free rice bread crumbs
½ cup Fluffy Cooked Quinoa,
  cooled
¼ cup Almond Flour Parm
2 tablespoons ghee or organic
  unsalted butter, melted
2 teaspoons Italian seasoning

Pasta and cheese—who would have thought that two simple ingredients would be such a delicious pair. This nostalgic comfort classic, updated with a crispy quinoa crust and creamy sweet potato cheese filling, is my answer to grown-up mac and cheese. Great as a weekend meal prep for weeknight dinners or leftover lunches for work.

1. Preheat the oven to 350°F.

2. Cook the macaroni in a large pot of boiling salted water until just tender, 9 to 11 minutes or according to package directions. Drain the pasta and rinse with cold water.

3. Return the pasta to the pot. Pour the Nacho Average Cheese Sauce over the pasta and stir well to coat. Spoon the pasta into a 9-inch pie plate or small casserole dish.

4. In a small bowl, toss together the bread crumbs, Fluffy Cooked Quinoa, Almond Flour Parm, ghee, and Italian seasoning. Sprinkle over the pasta.

5. Cover with foil and bake for 20 minutes. Remove the foil and broil for 5 to 7 minutes, until golden and crispy. Serve hot. Store any leftovers in an airtight container in the fridge for up to 4 days.

Smoky White Bean Kale Soup

Serves 4 to 6 • **Prep Time 10 minutes** • **Cook Time 30 to 35 minutes**

Ingredients

1 tablespoon extra-virgin olive oil

1 shallot, finely chopped

2 cloves garlic, minced

2 stalks celery, sliced

2 medium carrots, peeled and sliced

5 cups low-sodium vegetable stock

1 bay leaf

3 sprigs fresh thyme, leaves stripped
from the stems

1 teaspoon smoked sweet paprika

1 teaspoon sea salt

½ teaspoon black pepper

¼ to ½ teaspoon red chili flakes
(adjust to taste)

2 cans (19 ounces/540 mL each)
cannellini beans, rinsed and
drained (or 4 cups cooked
cannellini beans)

3 cups loosely packed stemmed
and roughly chopped kale

Juice of ½ lemon

This hearty, rustic soup is made with simple ingredients like kale and buttery white beans, cooked in a smoked paprika broth. Smoked paprika is amazing for adding a deep smoky flavour to your dishes. It adds heat but isn't spicy. This soup hits the spot on chilly fall days when you're cozied up on the couch with a blanket. Serve with crusty bread or my Everyday Nut and Seed Loaf (page 91).

1. In a large pot, heat the olive oil over medium heat. Add the shallot and garlic and cook for 1 to 2 minutes until fragrant. Add the celery and carrots and cook for 3 minutes, stirring frequently.

2. Pour in the vegetable stock, add the bay leaf, thyme, paprika, salt, black pepper, chili flakes, and cannellini beans, and bring to a gentle boil. Cover, reduce the heat to medium-low, and simmer for 25 to 30 minutes until the vegetables are cooked and tender, stirring halfway through.

3. Remove the bay leaf. Transfer 4 cups of the soup to a high-speed blender and purée for 10 seconds. Pour the puréed soup back into the pot. Stir in the kale and lemon juice and simmer for another 5 minutes.

4. Ladle the hot soup into bowls. Store any leftovers in an airtight container in the fridge for up to 1 week or in the freezer for up to 1 month.

🌰 **HEALTHNUT TIP** If you're looking to add this to your weekly meal prep, this recipe can easily be doubled and frozen into portioned containers for easy lunches or dinners throughout the week. Transfer the container to the fridge the night before to thaw, and heat up on the stove when ready to eat.

Quickie Turkey Chili

Serves 6 to 8 • Prep Time 10 minutes • Cook Time 25 to 30 minutes

Ingredients

1 tablespoon extra-virgin olive oil

1 yellow onion, chopped

3 cloves garlic, minced

1 pound (450 g) lean ground turkey

1 cup chopped zucchini

1 cup chopped cremini mushrooms

2 tablespoons tomato paste

1 tablespoon chili powder

1½ teaspoons chipotle chili powder

1 teaspoon sea salt

1 teaspoon ground cumin

½ teaspoon ground turmeric

½ teaspoon black pepper

1 cup low-sodium chicken stock
or vegetable stock

1 can (28 ounces/796 mL) diced
tomatoes

1 cup frozen corn kernels

1 cup canned refried black beans

1 can (14 ounces/398 mL) black
beans, rinsed and drained
(or 1½ cups cooked black beans)

1 can (14 ounces/398 mL) red
kidney beans, rinsed and drained
(or 1½ cups cooked red kidney
beans)

1 tablespoon pure maple syrup

2 teaspoons cinnamon

Fresh cilantro or sliced green onions
(white and light green parts only),
for garnish

Just thinking about a big bowl of chili makes me feel all warm and cozy. This hearty, veggie-packed, one-pot turkey chili is just the thing you need for cooler nights. I'm in love with the creamy thick base the refried beans give this chili! A little maple syrup balances out the acidity of the tomatoes, while the unexpected cinnamon adds a hint of Moroccan spice.

1. In a large pot, heat the olive oil over medium heat. Add the onion and garlic and cook until translucent, 1 to 2 minutes. Add the turkey and cook until evenly brown, breaking it up with a wooden spoon or spatula.

2. Add the zucchini, mushrooms, tomato paste, chili powder, chipotle chili powder, salt, cumin, turmeric, and black pepper. Give it a good stir and cook for 2 minutes.

3. Add the chicken stock, tomatoes, corn, refried black beans, black beans, and red kidney beans. Stir until well combined. Bring to a boil, reduce the heat to medium-low, and simmer for 20 minutes, stirring occasionally.

4. Stir in the maple syrup and cinnamon and simmer for another 5 minutes.

5. Ladle into bowls and serve garnished with cilantro. Store any leftovers in an airtight container in the fridge for up to 5 days or in the freezer for up to 1 month.

VARIATION If you're vegetarian, just leave out the ground turkey and add an extra cup or two of chopped mushrooms for an easy plant-based swap.

Korean Bibimbap

Serves 2 • Prep Time 15 minutes • Cook Time 18 to 20 minutes

Rice

1 cup white sushi rice, rinsed

2 cups water

Sauce

2 tablespoons sambal oelek
   (chili paste) or Sriracha

1 tablespoon water

1 tablespoon toasted sesame oil

1 tablespoon white miso paste

2 teaspoons pure liquid honey

1 teaspoon gluten-free tamari

1 teaspoon apple cider vinegar

Toppings

1½ teaspoons avocado oil

1 clove garlic, minced

2 cups tightly packed sliced
   shiitake mushrooms

2 baby bok choy, roughly chopped

2 Shanghai bok choy, roughly
   chopped

2 tablespoons water

2 cups bean sprouts

1 green onion (white and light
   green parts only), thinly sliced,
   divided

1 tablespoon gluten-free tamari

2 teaspoons toasted sesame oil

1 teaspoon apple cider vinegar

Sea salt

1 carrot, peeled and cut into
   matchsticks

1 tablespoon kimchi

2 Sunny-Side-Up Eggs (page 218)

2 teaspoons sesame seeds

The popular Korean dish bibimbap, which means "mixed rice," is a combination of cooked rice, sautéed vegetables, meat, egg, and a spicy red chili sauce. I swapped out the meat for sliced shiitake mushrooms, whose texture makes them a great meat replacement. I also created my own spicy red sauce made from ingredients like miso, chili paste, sesame oil, and tamari that brings this whole dish together when you mix it all up. This recipe is almost as much fun to eat as it is to pronounce, so grab your chopsticks and dig in!

1. Cook the Rice In a medium saucepan, combine the rice and water. Cover and bring to a boil, then reduce the heat to low and simmer until the rice is tender and the water is absorbed, about 10 minutes. Remove from the heat and let stand, covered, 10 minutes. (Alternatively, steam the rice in a rice cooker according to the manufacturer's instructions.) Keep warm.

2. Meanwhile, make the Sauce In a small food processor, combine the sambal oelek, water, sesame oil, miso, honey, tamari, and cider vinegar. Process for 5 seconds. Set aside.

3. Bring a medium saucepan of water to a boil.

4. Prepare the Toppings In a large skillet, heat the avocado oil over medium heat. Add the garlic and cook, stirring, for 1 minute. Add the mushrooms to one side of the skillet and on the other side add the bok choy. Add the water, cover, and cook for 8 to 10 minutes until the mushrooms are tender and the bok choy leaves turn bright green and the stalks are slightly translucent, stirring occasionally.

5. While the veggies are cooking, add the bean sprouts to the boiling water and blanch for 3 minutes. Remove to a colander with a slotted spoon and rinse under cold water for 5 to 10 seconds to stop the cooking, then drain. Transfer to a small bowl, add half the green onions, the tamari, sesame oil, cider vinegar, and a pinch of salt. Set aside.

6. Add the carrots to the boiling water and blanch for 3 minutes. Transfer to a plate with a slotted spoon.

7. To assemble, divide the rice between 2 big bowls. Arrange the mushrooms, bok choy, bean sprouts, and carrots nicely on top. Top with kimchi and a Sunny-Side-Up Egg and drizzle with the sauce. Sprinkle with sesame seeds and the remaining green onions and serve.

🌰 **HEALTHNUT TIP** Use up leftovers in your fridge to make your own version of this dish. Cooked quinoa, sautéed greens, or shredded cooked chicken breast can easily be used in your own DIY version of bibimbap.

Bali Mee Goreng

Serves 4 • **Prep Time 10 minutes** • **Cook Time 10 minutes**

Ingredients

2 packages (2½ ounces/70 g each)
  dried thin and wavy rice ramen
  noodles
1 tablespoon avocado oil
1 shallot, thinly sliced
2 cups chopped Chinese broccoli
2 cups finely shredded red cabbage
Sea salt and pepper
2 cups bean sprouts

Sweet and Spicy Soy Sauce

4 tablespoons gluten-free tamari
1 tablespoon blackstrap molasses
1 tablespoon sambal oelek
  (chili paste) or Sriracha
1 tablespoon pure liquid honey
2 teaspoons toasted sesame oil

Topping

4 Sunny-Side-Up Eggs (page 218)
1 green onion (white and light
  green parts only), thinly sliced

This popular Indonesian staple takes me back to Bali mornings and eating mee goreng for breakfast. I never thought I would be the girl to eat noodles for breakfast, but in many cultures breakfast is a savoury meal. So when in Rome—or in this case Bali—I ate copious amounts of spicy noodles and loved every mouthful! These fried noodles are sweet and slightly spicy, pack a ton of flavour, and are a great option for a quick weeknight dinner. You'll fall in love with every saucy noodle.

1. Cook the noodles in a large pot of boiling salted water according to the package directions. Drain the noodles and rinse under cold water.

2. Meanwhile, make the Sweet and Spicy Soy Sauce In a small bowl, whisk together the tamari, molasses, sambal oelek, honey, and sesame oil.

3. In a large wok or skillet, heat the avocado oil over medium-high heat. Add the shallot and stir-fry for 1 minute. Add the broccoli, red cabbage, and a pinch each of salt and pepper and stir-fry for 2 minutes. Stir in the Sweet and Spicy Soy Sauce, cover, reduce the heat to medium, and cook for 2 minutes. Add the cooked noodles and the bean sprouts, toss everything together using tongs, and cook for 2 to 3 minutes until the sauce has slightly thickened and the noodles are well coated.

4. Serve on plates with a Sunny-Side-Up egg on top and sprinkled with green onions. Store any leftovers (without the egg) in an airtight container in the fridge for up to 4 days.

HEALTHNUT TIP Chinese broccoli, also known as gai lan, can be hard to find at large grocery stores, so check out your local Asian market. Alternatively, you can substitute broccolini or rapini.

Spring Veggie Quiche Tarts

Makes four 4-inch tarts • Prep Time 10 minutes • Bake Time 35 minutes

. . . .

Prep Ahead

Spelt Pastry Dough (page 221)

Ingredients

1 batch Spelt Pastry Dough

4 eggs

1 clove garlic, minced

½ cup unsweetened almond milk or
   coconut milk (from the carton)

2 tablespoons chopped fresh
   flat-leaf parsley

Zest of ½ lemon

1 tablespoon fresh lemon juice

½ teaspoon sea salt

¼ teaspoon pepper

½ cup fresh or frozen peas

2 tablespoons chopped sun-dried
   tomatoes

1 tablespoon crumbled soft
   goat cheese

Just looking at these individual quiches makes me think of spring! The buttery, flaky crust is light and airy and the perfect base for the lemony pea-flecked filling. The fresh parsley, sun-dried tomatoes, and salty tang from the goat cheese make every bite a burst of refreshing flavours. Serve with a tossed mixed green salad or my Fennel Citrus Kale Salad (page 115) and you've got the perfect meal.

1. Preheat the oven to 400°F.

2. To prepare the tart shells, using your hands, knead the Spelt Pastry Dough into a ball. Divide the dough into 4 equal pieces. On a floured work surface, roll out each piece of dough into a 5-inch circle about ¼ inch thick. Transfer each dough circle to a 4-inch round tart pan with removable bottom, pressing it onto the bottom and up the sides. Line each shell with a square of parchment paper and fill with pie weights or dried beans. Put on a baking sheet and bake for 10 minutes. Remove the parchment and pie weights. Reduce the oven to 375°F.

3. To make the filling, in a medium bowl, combine the eggs, garlic, almond milk, parsley, lemon zest, lemon juice, salt, and pepper; whisk until well combined. Add the peas, sun-dried tomatoes, and goat cheese and stir to combine. Pour the filling into the tart shells.

4. Bake the quiches for 25 minutes, or until the crust is golden and the filling is firm to the touch. Let cool in the pans for 5 minutes, then remove the sides. Serve warm. Store any leftovers in an airtight container in the fridge for up to 1 week or in the freezer for up to 1 month.

VARIATION If you don't have small tart pans, you can make 8 quiche cups using a muffin tin. Cut out dough circles using a 5-inch round cookie cutter. Preheat the oven to 350°F. Poke the bottom and side of the dough with a fork and bake for 5 minutes. Divide the filling among the cups and bake for about 20 minutes, until the crust is golden and the filling is firm to the touch. You can also make this in a 9-inch pie plate; extend the filling baking time to 30 minutes.

HEALTHNUT TIP Once you use beans or lentils for prebaking ("blind baking") your tart shells, you won't be able to use them for cooking, so just pop them into a jar and save them for your next baking day.

Zucchini Corn Fritters

Makes 8 patties • Prep Time 10 minutes • Cook Time 12 minutes

Cumin Yogurt Dip

½ cup plain full-fat yogurt or
coconut yogurt

2 teaspoons ground cumin

Sea salt

Zucchini Corn Fritters

¼ cup unsweetened soy milk

1½ teaspoons apple cider vinegar

2 medium zucchini, grated
(about 3½ cups grated)

½ cup chickpea flour

½ cup oat flour

½ teaspoon baking soda

½ teaspoon smoked paprika

½ teaspoon sea salt

¼ teaspoon black pepper

¼ teaspoon ground cumin

2 cloves garlic, minced

1 cup fresh or thawed frozen
corn kernels, patted dry

¼ cup finely chopped red onion

1 tablespoon chopped seeded
cayenne chili pepper

1 egg, lightly beaten

2 to 3 tablespoons avocado oil,
for frying

Hearty yet simple, these flavourful fritters are packed with spices, grated zucchini, and sweet corn to enjoy as either an appetizer or a light lunch with a side salad. I use chickpea flour—naturally gluten-free and full of fibre and protein—because it is a fantastic binder for fritters or burgers. Serve these warm with a side of cooling sauce like this Cumin Yogurt Dip or my Not-So-Basic Guacamole (page 82).

1. Make the Cumin Yogurt Dip In a small bowl, whisk together the yogurt, cumin, and a pinch of sea salt. Cover and refrigerate until ready to use. Dip can be stored in an airtight container in the fridge for up to 4 days.

2. Make the Zucchini Corn Fritters Combine the soy milk and cider vinegar in a small glass bowl and set aside for 5 minutes to curdle.

3. Wrap the zucchini in a kitchen towel and twist to wring out all the excess liquid.

4. In a small bowl, whisk together the chickpea flour, oat flour, baking soda, paprika, salt, black pepper, and cumin.

5. In a medium bowl, combine the grated zucchini, garlic, corn, onion, and chili pepper; give it a quick toss to mix. Add the dry ingredients and stir until well combined. Pour in the curdled soy milk and the egg and stir until well combined.

6. In a large non-stick skillet, heat 2 tablespoons of the avocado oil over medium heat. Scoop ¼ cup of the fritter mixture at a time and form into ¼-inch-thick patties. Working in batches if necessary, fry for 2 to 3 minutes per side, until crispy and golden brown. Repeat until all patties are cooked, adding more avocado oil if needed.

7. Serve immediately with the Cumin Yogurt Dip. Store any leftover cooled fritters in an airtight container in the fridge for up to 5 days or transfer to a resealable freezer bag and store in the freezer for up to 1 month.

Spiralized Zucchini Nests with Poached Eggs

Serves 4 • **Prep Time 10 minutes** • **Cook Time 10 minutes**

Ingredients

1 tablespoon extra-virgin olive oil

1 cup quartered cremini mushrooms

1 clove garlic, chopped

2 medium zucchini, spiralized

Sea salt and pepper

4 eggs

1 large ripe avocado, pitted,
   peeled, and sliced

I love that you can now buy pre-spiralized produce in grocery stores. You don't even need to own a spiralizer—which makes me wonder why I own three! These zucchini nests with poached eggs are a staple lunch for me: not only do they resemble noodles, which is always fun, but they soak up any flavour you add to them. I love that this dish can be cooked in one pan, so cleanup is super easy.

1. In a large non-stick skillet, heat the olive oil over medium heat. Add the mushrooms and garlic and cook, stirring frequently, for 2 to 3 minutes until tender.

2. Add the spiralized zucchini and a pinch each of salt and pepper. Cook for 2 to 3 minutes, until the zucchini is slightly softened but still firm on the inside, stirring occasionally. Using a wooden spoon, divide the zucchini into 4 equal portions or "nests" and create a well in each. Crack 1 egg into each well and season with a pinch each of salt and pepper. Cover and cook for 4 to 5 minutes, until the egg whites are cooked and no longer translucent but the yolk is still slightly runny.

3. Serve immediately, garnished with avocado slices.

VARIATION Swap out the zucchini for spiralized sweet potato. Add thinly sliced red onion to the mushrooms and garlic mixture for extra flavour.

HEALTHNUT TIP I like to spiralize 4 to 6 medium zucchini in advance and store them in an airtight container in the fridge for up to 5 days to throw in recipes on the fly.

Roasted Poblano and Mushroom Fajitas

Serves 4 to 6 • Prep Time 15 minutes • Cook Time 20 minutes

Kale Cabbage Slaw

2 cups packed stemmed and
   shredded black kale
2 cups packed shredded red
   cabbage
Juice of ½ lemon
1½ teaspoons pure liquid honey
¼ teaspoon sea salt

Veggie Filling

2 tablespoons avocado oil
1 tablespoon fresh lemon juice
1½ teaspoons gluten-free tamari
½ teaspoon ground coriander
½ teaspoon smoked sweet paprika
½ teaspoon garlic powder
¼ teaspoon ground cumin
¼ teaspoon sea salt
¼ teaspoon black pepper
2 portobello mushrooms,
   stemmed and thinly sliced
2 poblano peppers, seeded
   and thinly sliced into strips
½ medium red onion,
   thinly sliced into strips
1 tablespoon seeded and finely
   diced red cayenne chili pepper

Avocado Sauce

1 large avocado, pitted and peeled
½ cup water
¼ cup chopped fresh cilantro
Juice of ½ lemon
1 clove garlic, chopped
Sea salt and pepper

For Serving

4 to 6 small soft corn tortillas
¼ cup crumbled feta cheese
Chopped fresh cilantro

My other half, Matt's, favourite cuisine, hands down, is Mexican, so anything taco-, nacho-, or in this case fajita-related is a crowd-pleaser in our home. Whether you're looking to up your Taco Tuesday game or just looking for an epic dinner recipe, these are it. You might be thinking, "Mushrooms and peppers . . . where's the beef?" The portobello mushrooms not only soak up all the flavours but will please both vegetarians and meat-eaters with their hearty and "meaty" texture. Roasted with the mildly spicy poblano pepper, this is a match made in fajita heaven. Oh, and don't be fooled: green poblano peppers may look like the common sweet green pepper, but they have a completely different taste. Roasting intensifies the deep flavour of the poblanos, adding a distinctive kick.

1. Preheat the oven to 400°F. Line a baking sheet with parchment paper.

2. Make the Kale Cabbage Slaw In a medium bowl, combine the kale, cabbage, lemon juice, honey, and salt. Massage with clean hands for 3 to 4 minutes to soften the kale and cabbage. Set aside in the fridge.

3. Prepare the Veggie Filling In a small bowl, whisk together the avocado oil, lemon juice, tamari, coriander, paprika, garlic powder, cumin, salt, and pepper. Put the mushrooms, poblano peppers, onion, and chili pepper on the prepared baking sheet, drizzle with the spice mixture, and toss well to coat. Roast for 20 minutes, turning halfway through.

4. In the last 5 minutes of roasting time, wrap the tortillas in foil and place in the oven to warm up.

5. Make the Avocado Sauce In a small food processor, combine the avocado, water, cilantro, lemon juice, garlic, and a pinch each of salt and pepper. Process for 5 to 10 seconds, until smooth.

6. Transfer the veggies to a serving bowl or platter. Serve with the warmed tortillas, Kale Cabbage Slaw, Avocado Sauce, cheese, and cilantro.

🌰 HEALTHNUT TIP If you're packing this up for leftovers or lunches, store the filling separately from the tortillas and assemble when ready to eat.

Saucy Cashew Chicken Lettuce Cups

Serves 4 to 5 • **Prep Time 20 minutes** • **Cook Time 10 minutes**

Ingredients

2 tablespoons pure liquid honey

2 tablespoons gluten-free tamari

1 tablespoon unseasoned rice
vinegar

1½ teaspoons sambal oelek
(chili paste) or Sriracha

1 teaspoon grated peeled
fresh ginger

1 teaspoon toasted sesame oil

1 teaspoon arrowroot flour

1 pound (450 g) boneless, skinless
chicken breast, cut into
1-inch cubes

1 tablespoon avocado oil

1 cup whole raw cashews

1 tablespoon thinly sliced seeded
cayenne chili pepper

2 green onions (white and light
green parts only), thinly sliced,
divided

2 teaspoons sesame seeds, divided

Sea salt and pepper

8 to 10 butter lettuce leaves

1 carrot, peeled into ribbons

Squeeze of fresh lime juice

These "better than takeout" cashew chicken lettuce wraps are so simple to prepare and are on the table in 30 minutes! They are sweet and spicy at the same time, with a pop of crunch from the whole cashews. Your taste buds will dance over the flavour with every mouth-watering bite. Perfect for busy weeknight dinners or to pack up for lunch.

1. In a large wide-mouth glass jar, combine the honey, tamari, rice vinegar, sambal oelek, ginger, sesame oil, and arrowroot flour. Cover and give it a good shake. Add the chicken and shake until the chicken is well coated. Cover and refrigerate for 15 minutes to marinate.

2. In a large non-stick skillet, heat the avocado oil over medium-high heat. Add the chicken with its marinade, cover, and cook for 5 minutes. Add the cashews, chili pepper, and half of the green onions. Cook, uncovered, for another 5 minutes, stirring occasionally. Remove from the heat, add 1 teaspoon of the sesame seeds and a pinch each of salt and pepper. Stir, then leave the chicken to cool for 5 minutes.

3. To assemble the lettuce wraps, top each lettuce leaf with 3 or 4 carrot ribbons and ¼ cup cashew chicken filling. Top with the remaining 1 teaspoon of sesame seeds, the remaining green onions, and a squeeze of lime. Store leftover chicken in an airtight container in the fridge for up to 4 days.

VARIATION You can swap out the chicken for tofu to make this veggie friendly or for Meatless Monday.

HEALTHNUT TIP If taking to work or school for lunch, package the filling and lettuce separately and assemble when you are ready to eat.

Baked Crispy Quinoa Chicken Fingers

Serves 6 to 8 (18 to 20 strips) • Prep Time 15 minutes • Bake Time 20 to 25 minutes

Prep Ahead
Fluffy Cooked Quinoa (page 219)

Maple Dijon Sauce
(makes ½ cup)

¼ cup plain full-fat yogurt or
   coconut yogurt
2 tablespoons grainy Dijon mustard
1 tablespoon pure maple syrup
¼ teaspoon ground turmeric
Sea salt

Baked Crispy Quinoa Chicken Fingers

4 skinless, boneless chicken breasts
   (8 ounces/225 g each)
½ cup oat flour
2 eggs
2 cups packed Fluffy Cooked Quinoa
½ cup gluten-free rice bread crumbs
1 tablespoon nutritional yeast
2 teaspoons Italian seasoning
1 teaspoon garlic powder
½ teaspoon sea salt
¼ teaspoon pepper

HEALTHNUT TIP When coating the chicken fingers, keep one hand for dry and one hand for wet. That way, the coatings won't stick to your fingers.

The popular childhood favourite with a grown-up twist: chicken fingers coated in a mix of rice bread crumbs and cooked quinoa for the ultimate crispy coating, baked to perfection in the oven. Great as a weeknight dinner or packed in your lunch box. Dip them in my Maple Dijon Sauce and serve with a side of baked sweet spuds, and I call that a healthy "happy meal"—no toy included.

1. Preheat the oven to 450°F. Line a baking sheet with parchment paper and spray with coconut oil.

2. **Make the Maple Dijon Sauce** In a small bowl, whisk together the yogurt, mustard, maple syrup, turmeric, and a pinch of salt. Set aside.

3. **Make the Baked Crispy Quinoa Chicken Fingers** Slice the chicken breasts lengthwise in half, then into four or five 1½-inch-wide strips. Set aside.

4. Put the oat flour in a shallow bowl. In a second shallow bowl, whisk the eggs. In a third shallow bowl, combine the Fluffy Cooked Quinoa, bread crumbs, nutritional yeast, Italian seasoning, garlic powder, salt, and pepper; mix well (I find using my hands works best).

5. Dredge each chicken strip in the oat flour, shaking off any excess, then dip into the egg, letting any excess drip off. Then dredge in the quinoa mixture, making sure to pat each chicken strip well into the quinoa mixture to evenly coat. Arrange the coated chicken strips in a single layer on the prepared baking sheet.

6. Bake for 10 to 12 minutes until the crust is crispy and golden on top. Carefully turn the chicken strips with a spatula and bake for an additional 10 minutes, or until golden and crispy. Serve hot with the Maple Dijon Sauce on the side for dipping. Store any leftover chicken strips and sauce in an airtight container in the fridge for up to 4 days.

VARIATION You can fry the chicken fingers on the stovetop instead of baking them. In a large non-stick skillet, heat 1 tablespoon of avocado oil or grapeseed oil over medium-high heat. Add the breaded chicken strips and cook for 5 to 6 minutes, until the crust begins to brown. Turn and cook for another 5 to 6 minutes, until the crust is brown and the chicken is cooked through and no longer translucent.

Chicken Crunch Wrap with Ranch

Serves 2 • Prep Time 10 minutes

Prep Ahead

Avocado Ranch Dip (page 229)

Baked Crispy Quinoa Chicken
Fingers (page 180)

Ingredients

4 to 6 tablespoons Avocado
Ranch Dip

2 large whole grain tortillas
or gluten-free wraps

4 romaine lettuce leaves

4 tomato slices

2 to 4 Baked Crispy Quinoa
Chicken Fingers

Fun ironic fact: my first part-time job was at KFC. Yes, your green-smoothie-drinking health nut used to serve fried chicken at a fast-food drive-thru. This epic non-deep-fried crispy chicken crunch wrap takes me back to those days and satisfies my fast-food cravings. Yes, I'm human and get those cravings, too. The mix of fresh tomatoes and lettuce with the tangy Avocado Ranch Dip, paired with crispy quinoa chicken, hits the spot every time. I love enjoying a wrap or two for lunch loaded with my ranch dip.

1. Spread 2 to 3 tablespoons Avocado Ranch Dip on each tortilla, then top with 2 lettuce leaves, 2 tomato slices, and 1 or 2 Baked Crispy Quinoa Chicken Fingers. Fold in the sides and roll up burrito style.

VARIATION   You can grill the wraps in a panini press or grill pan over medium-high heat. Brush the pan with 1 teaspoon of avocado oil and grill the wraps for 2 to 3 minutes on each side for an outer crunch. You can also swap out the Avocado Ranch Dip for my Maple Dijon Sauce (page 230).

HEALTHNUT TIP   If you don't have time to cook up a batch of my Baked Crispy Quinoa Chicken Fingers (page 180), you can use grilled chicken cut into strips instead.

Maple "Baked" Beans

Makes 4 cups • Prep Time 5 minutes • Cook Time 25 minutes

Ingredients

1 shallot, roughly chopped

1 clove garlic, roughly chopped

2 teaspoons extra-virgin olive oil

3 tablespoons pure maple syrup

1 tablespoon tomato paste

1 tablespoon blackstrap molasses

1 tablespoon apple cider vinegar

2 cans (19 ounces/540 mL each)
   navy or pinto beans, rinsed and
   drained (or 4 cups cooked navy
   or pinto beans)

1 cup water

¼ teaspoon sea salt

¼ teaspoon pepper

Heinz baked beans were a staple and a favourite of mine when I was a kid. I would ask my mom for beans with a fried egg on the side almost every day. As an adult, I still love my baked beans, but I healthified my childhood favourite with simple, wholesome ingredients. The blackstrap molasses and maple syrup give these beans a rich, deep flavour. They'll taste like they've been cooking for hours, when in fact they take only 30 minutes! I love making a batch during my Sunday meal prep, then enjoying them with my meals throughout the week as an easy and tasty source of protein and fibre.

1. In a small food processor, blitz the shallot and garlic for 5 seconds, or until finely minced. This will help them melt into the beans while still adding a punch of flavour.

2. Heat the olive oil in a medium saucepan over medium heat. Add the shallot and garlic mixture and cook for 1 minute, stirring.

3. Add the maple syrup, tomato paste, molasses, and cider vinegar; stir to combine. Add the beans, water, salt, and pepper and bring to a boil. Reduce the heat to medium-low and simmer, uncovered, for 25 minutes, stirring occasionally to prevent the beans from sticking to the bottom of the pot.

4. Serve warm as a side dish, spooned on a baked potato or toast, or my favourite, with a fried egg. Store any leftovers in an airtight container in the fridge for up to 1 week.

SWEETS

Fudgy Peanut Butter Cookies

Makes 14 cookies • **Prep Time 5 minutes** • **Chill Time 15 minutes** • **Bake Time 10 to 11 minutes**

Ingredients

1 cup natural smooth (not drippy)
   peanut butter, refrigerated
   until solid

1 egg, lightly beaten

½ cup pure maple syrup

1 teaspoon pure vanilla extract

½ cup oat flour

¼ teaspoon sea salt (omit if using
   salted peanut butter)

I know chocolate chip cookies get all the attention, but trust me when I say that the peanut butter cookie is going to have a comeback when you sink your teeth into these new and improved sweet gems. Some of the best foods are beige—think croissants, doughnuts, bread, pasta, peanut butter. See a theme here? Made in one bowl, these soft, chewy, and fudgy-centred cookies have the right combination of salty and sweet. Serve them with a tall glass of cold almond milk, and you have yourself the perfect mid-afternoon treat!

1. Preheat the oven to 350°F. Line a baking sheet with parchment paper.

2. In a medium bowl, combine the peanut butter, egg, maple syrup, and vanilla. Stir together with a rubber spatula until smooth. Fold in the oat flour and salt (if using) until well combined and no flour is visible.

3. Form the dough into a ball, cover with plastic wrap, and chill in the freezer for about 15 minutes to firm up.

4. Roll 1½ tablespoons of the dough at a time into 1-inch balls. Place the balls about 2 inches apart on the prepared baking sheet. Flatten the balls with the back of a fork so they are half as high as they were.

5. Bake for 10 to 11 minutes, until the bottoms are slightly golden. Let the cookies cool on the baking sheet for 2 or 3 minutes before transferring to a rack to cool completely. Store in an airtight container at room temperature for up to 1 week or in the freezer for up to 1 month.

VARIATION For a nut-free and school-friendly version, use sunflower seed butter instead of peanut butter.

New-Fashioned Chocolate Chip Cookies

Makes 12 to 14 cookies • Prep Time 10 minutes • Bake Time 10 to 12 minutes

Ingredients

1½ cups light spelt flour

1 teaspoon baking soda

½ teaspoon baking powder

¼ teaspoon sea salt

¾ cup coconut sugar

½ cup solid coconut oil

2 teaspoons pure vanilla extract

1 egg

½ cup semi-sweet chocolate chips
(dairy-free, if required)

Most of us love the classic old-fashioned chocolate chip cookie we grew up with. Well, let me introduce you to these new and improved, fresh-off-the-baking-sheet "new-fashioned" cookies. These soft and chewy cookies with crisp edges are sure to satisfy any sweet cravings. These just go to prove that healthier options don't have to taste healthier; they can taste just as good—if not better. So grab your glass of almond milk and show me your best cookie dip.

1. Preheat the oven to 350°F. Line a baking sheet with parchment paper.

2. In a large bowl, stir together the spelt flour, baking soda, baking powder, and salt.

3. In a medium bowl, with a hand-held electric mixer, beat the coconut sugar with the coconut oil for 2 minutes on medium speed. Scrape down the sides, add the vanilla and egg, and beat for 30 seconds.

4. Add the coconut oil mixture to the flour mixture and stir with a rubber spatula or wooden spoon until well combined and no flour is visible. Fold in the chocolate chips.

5. Roll about 1½ tablespoons of the mixture at a time into balls. Place them about 1 inch apart on the prepared baking sheet.

6. Bake for 10 to 12 minutes, until golden. Transfer the cookies to a rack to cool completely. Store in an airtight container at room temperature for up to 3 days or in the fridge for up to 5 days, or in a resealable freezer bag in the freezer for up to 1 month.

Raw Chocolate Chip Cookie Dough Bites

Makes 10 bites • **Prep Time 10 minutes**

Ingredients

½ cup natural cashew butter

2 tablespoons pure maple syrup

½ teaspoon pure vanilla extract

¾ cup almond flour

¼ teaspoon sea salt

¼ cup semi-sweet chocolate chips
(dairy-free, if required)

We've all bought a tube of cookie dough because we were going to bake cookies but ended up eating it raw, straight out of the package. (C'mon, admit it!) And because "eating" and "regret" should never be in the same sentence together, I decided to make a healthified cookie dough that you can eat raw and is also an energizing snack high in protein and healthy fats. What is it about raw cookie dough, anyway? Is it the soft texture, the salty-sweet buttery flavour, or the guilty pleasure we get from eating something we're not "supposed" to? Now you can eat your cookie dough—guilt-free!

1. In a medium bowl, stir together the cashew butter, maple syrup, and vanilla. Add the almond flour and salt and stir until a dough forms. Fold in the chocolate chips.

2. Roll about 1½ tablespoons of the mixture at a time into balls. Enjoy right away as a snack or dessert, or store in an airtight container in the fridge for up to 1 week or in the freezer for up to 1 month.

🥜 **HEALTHNUT TIP** I like using my handy 1½-inch ice-cream scoop for easy scooping and rolling.

Lemon-Glazed Blueberry Muffins

Makes 12 muffins • **Prep Time 10 minutes** • **Bake Time 22 to 25 minutes**

Prep Ahead

Coconut Butter Lemon Glaze
   (page 232)

Ingredients

Juice of ½ lemon

½ cup unsweetened soy milk

2 cups light spelt flour

1 teaspoon baking powder

½ teaspoon sea salt

1¼ cups fresh or frozen blueberries,
   divided

2 eggs

½ cup pure liquid honey

⅓ cup coconut oil, melted

1 teaspoon pure vanilla extract

Zest of 1 lemon

½ cup Coconut Butter Lemon Glaze

Fluffy, lemony muffins filled with bursts of blueberries and finished with a coconut butter lemon glaze that'll make your taste buds love you. It's healthy enough to have for breakfast, but also sweet enough for dessert. The choice is yours! Add these to your weekly meal prep so you can have healthy baked treats on demand throughout the week.

1. Preheat the oven to 350°F. Line a muffin tin with 12 paper liners.

2. In a measuring cup, stir the lemon juice into the soy milk and set aside for about 5 minutes to curdle. This will create a non-dairy "buttermilk."

3. In a large bowl, whisk together the spelt flour, baking powder, and salt. Add 1 cup of the blueberries and give it a quick stir.

4. In a medium bowl, combine the eggs, honey, coconut oil, vanilla, soy milk mixture, and lemon zest. Beat until well combined. Pour the egg mixture into the flour mixture and stir with a rubber spatula until well combined, trying not to overmix.

5. Fill each muffin cup with about ¼ cup of the batter. (I like using a large ice-cream scoop to get an even measure.) Firmly press 2 or 3 of the remaining blueberries into the top of each muffin.

6. Bake for 22 to 25 minutes, until a toothpick inserted in the centre comes out clean. Let muffins sit for 5 minutes before turning out onto a rack to cool.

7. Once the muffins are almost cool, drizzle 1 to 2 teaspoons of Coconut Butter Lemon Glaze over each muffin. Store any leftovers in an airtight container at room temperature for 2 to 3 days or in the fridge for up to 1 week.

VARIATION You can use other berries like raspberries for another yummy option!

🌰 **HEALTHNUT TIP** I like to make my own "buttermilk" because I don't use it much and don't want to buy a whole carton. This way I can make the exact amount I need for each recipe.

One-Bowl Carrot Cake Muffins

Makes 12 muffins • Prep Time 10 minutes • Bake Time 18 to 20 minutes

Ingredients

1 cup unsweetened almond milk
   or soy milk
1 teaspoon apple cider vinegar
¾ cup coconut sugar
½ cup unsweetened applesauce
¼ cup coconut oil, melted
1 teaspoon pure vanilla extract
2 eggs
2 cups spelt flour
½ cup almond flour
1 teaspoon cinnamon
1 teaspoon baking soda
½ teaspoon sea salt
¼ teaspoon ground nutmeg
1 cup peeled and grated carrots
   (about 2 small carrots)

Topping

½ cup raw walnuts, roughly
   chopped
1 tablespoon coconut sugar

I love that carrot cake isn't just for Easter, because if I can sneak some veggies into my dessert and still have it taste sweet and delicious, I'm all in any day of the year! I never used to be a fan of carrot cake, I think because I had only tried the store-bought ones loaded with so much sugar that you can't detect any carrot. Since making my own version using unrefined sugar and wholesome ingredients, I have officially been converted. Sweet and perfectly spiced, these carrot cake muffins are so good, even the Easter Bunny would approve.

1. Preheat the oven to 375°F. Line a muffin tin with 12 paper liners.

2. In a measuring cup, whisk together the almond milk and cider vinegar and set aside for 5 minutes to curdle. This will create a non-dairy "buttermilk."

3. In a large bowl, whisk together the coconut sugar, applesauce, coconut oil, vanilla, and eggs. Pour in the almond milk mixture and whisk to combine. Sift in the spelt flour, almond flour, cinnamon, baking soda, salt, and nutmeg; whisk until the batter is smooth. Fold in the grated carrots until combined.

4. Fill each muffin cup with about ¼ cup of batter. Top each muffin with chopped walnuts and sprinkle with coconut sugar.

5. Bake for 18 to 20 minutes, until a toothpick inserted in the centre comes out clean. Let muffins sit for 5 minutes before turning out onto a rack to cool completely. Store in an airtight container at room temperature for up to 3 days or in the fridge for up to 5 days.

HEALTHNUT TIP Allow the muffins to fully cool before removing the paper liners or else it will stick to the paper.

Almond Swirl Chocolate Brownies

Makes 9 brownies • Prep Time 10 minutes • Bake Time 22 to 25 minutes

Ingredients

3½ ounces (100 g) semi-sweet baking chocolate, roughly chopped

⅓ cup coconut oil

½ cup coconut sugar

½ cup + 1 to 2 tablespoons natural smooth almond butter, divided

1 teaspoon pure vanilla extract

2 eggs

2 tablespoons coconut flour

½ teaspoon baking soda

¼ teaspoon salt (omit if using salted almond butter)

¼ cup dairy-free semi-sweet chocolate chips

Soft and moist cake-like brownies made without dairy, processed sugar, or even flour! After many attempts (seven, to be exact) at the perfect chocolaty, nutty brownie, I think I've nailed it. I may have eaten my weight in brownies while taste-testing this recipe, but I'm not complaining! The secret to these brownies is melted chocolate, healthy fats from the coconut oil, and a rich almond butter swirl on top that just melts in your mouth with every chocolaty bite. Serve warm with Coconut Whip (page 231) or a scoop of vanilla ice cream.

1. Preheat the oven to 350°F. Line an 8-inch square baking pan with parchment paper, leaving an overhang at the sides to allow for easy removal after cooling.

2. Combine the baking chocolate and coconut oil in a heatproof bowl and set over (not in) a saucepan of simmering water. Whisk slowly until the chocolate is melted. Remove from the heat and transfer to a large bowl. Add the coconut sugar, ½ cup of the almond butter, vanilla, and eggs and whisk until smooth.

3. Add the coconut flour, baking soda, and salt (if using) and stir until well combined and the batter is thick and fudgy. Fold in the chocolate chips.

4. Scrape the batter into the prepared pan and level the top with a spatula. Spoon the remaining 1 to 2 tablespoons almond butter in random dollops on top of the batter. Drag the back of a knife through the almond butter to make a swirl pattern.

5. Bake for 22 to 25 minutes, until the edges are starting to firm up. The middle will be soft to the touch and will look slightly sunken. Let the brownies cool in the pan on a rack for 10 to 15 minutes before lifting out with the parchment paper. Cut into 2½-inch squares and serve warm or cooled. Store any leftovers in an airtight container at room temperature for up to 3 days or in the fridge for up to 1 week.

🌰 **HEALTHNUT TIP** Coconut flour is not only gluten-free but budget friendly: because it is super absorbent, you need only a small amount in recipes.

Cherry Almond Jubilee Galettes

Makes four 4-inch galettes • **Prep Time 10 minutes** • **Bake Time 22 to 25 minutes**

Prep Ahead

Spelt Pastry Dough (page 221)

Ingredients

3 cups fresh or thawed frozen
    pitted sweet cherries

2 tablespoons arrowroot flour

2 tablespoons pure maple syrup

1 teaspoon pure almond extract

¼ teaspoon nutmeg

Zest of 1 orange

Juice of ¼ orange

Sea salt

1 batch Spelt Pastry Dough

2½ teaspoons coconut sugar,
    divided

1 egg

½ tablespoon water

3 tablespoons sliced blanched
    almonds

These rustic, flaky cherry-filled French tarts are the perfect excuse to use up your favourite summer fruit. The hint of orange and almond, combined with the sweetness of the fruit, creates the most mouth-watering dessert—you'll definitely want seconds! I love enjoying this galette warm with a scoop of dairy-free vanilla ice cream and a cup of tea, or cooled with my Coconut Butter Lemon Glaze (page 232) drizzled on top.

1. Preheat the oven to 400°F. Line a baking sheet with parchment paper.

2. To make the cherry almond filling, in a medium bowl, combine the cherries, arrowroot flour, maple syrup, almond extract, nutmeg, orange zest, orange juice, and a pinch of salt. Stir well and set aside.

3. Using your hands, knead the Spelt Pastry Dough into a ball. Divide the dough into 4 equal pieces. On a floured work surface, roll out each piece of dough into a 6-inch circle about ¼ inch thick. Gently transfer each dough round to the prepared baking sheet and sprinkle each with ½ teaspoon of the coconut sugar.

4. In a small bowl, whisk together the egg and water to make an egg wash. Brush the edges of the dough with the egg wash. Divide the fruit filling among the pastry circles, slightly mounding it in the middle and leaving a 1-inch border around the edge. Fold the dough border up and over the edge of the filling, overlapping the dough as you go around, and pleating the dough, using egg wash in between as needed to help it stick together. Brush dough with egg wash. Sprinkle galettes with the remaining ½ teaspoon coconut sugar and the sliced almonds.

5. Bake for 22 to 25 minutes, until the galettes are golden brown and the juices are bubbling. Let cool on the baking sheet for about 5 minutes before transferring to a rack.

VARIATION This recipe also works great with blueberries, mixed berries, or sliced stone fruits such as apricots or peaches.

Strawberry Rhubarb Hand Pies

Makes 8 hand pies • Prep Time 15 minutes • Bake Time 20 to 25 minutes

Prep Ahead
Spelt Pastry Dough (page 221)
Coconut Butter Lemon Glaze
(page 232)

Ingredients
1½ cups fresh strawberries,
chopped
½ cup fresh rhubarb, chopped
2 tablespoons arrowroot flour
3 tablespoons coconut sugar,
divided
1 teaspoon pure vanilla extract
1 batch Spelt Pastry Dough
1 egg
½ tablespoon water
½ cup Coconut Butter Lemon Glaze

Fresh strawberries and rhubarb wrapped in a flaky pastry. Really, is there anything better? I used to never eat strawberry rhubarb pies because the ones I found at most grocery stores were full of sugars and syrups, with barely any fruit. These cute, portable hand pies, on the other hand, are stuffed to the edges with five simple ingredients you can feel good about eating for dessert—or breakfast, I'm not judging! I love enjoying a couple warm out of the oven drizzled (drenched) with my Coconut Lemon Butter Glaze (page 232).

1. Preheat the oven to 400°F. Line a baking sheet with parchment paper.

2. To make the strawberry rhubarb filling, in a medium bowl, combine the strawberries, rhubarb, arrowroot flour, 2 tablespoons of the coconut sugar, and vanilla. Stir well and set aside.

3. Using your hands, knead the Spelt Pastry Dough into a ball. Divide the dough into 2 equal pieces. Wrap one piece in plastic wrap and return to the refrigerator. On a floured work surface, roll out the dough until ⅛ inch thick. Using a 4½-inch round cookie cutter, cut out circles, rerolling dough scraps as needed. Repeat with the other portion of dough to make 8 circles.

4. In a small bowl, whisk together the egg and water to make an egg wash. Brush the edges of each pastry round with the egg wash and sprinkle a little coconut sugar in the middle.

5. Spoon 1½ tablespoons of the strawberry rhubarb filling over the bottom half of a pastry round, leaving a 1-inch border. Fold the top half of the round over the filling to create a half-moon shape and press the edges down firmly with your fingers. Then use a fork to press down on the edges to seal the pie. Transfer to the prepared baking sheet. Repeat with the remaining filling and pastry rounds. Cut 3 slits in the top of each pie with a sharp knife. Brush the pie tops with egg wash and sprinkle each pie with a pinch of coconut sugar.

6. Bake for 20 to 25 minutes, until golden brown. Transfer to a rack and let cool for 10 minutes.

7. While warm, drizzle with Coconut Butter Lemon Glaze and enjoy. Store any leftovers in an airtight container at room temperature for up to 2 days or in the fridge for up to 5 days.

Key Lime Pie in a Jar

Makes six 8-ounce jars • Prep Time 15 minutes • Cook Time 30 minutes • Chill Time 4 hours or overnight

Prep Ahead
Coconut Whip (page 231)

Crust
1 cup old-fashioned rolled oats

1 cup unsalted raw pecan halves

¼ cup unsweetened shredded coconut

¼ teaspoon cinnamon

¼ teaspoon sea salt

¼ cup coconut oil, melted

1 tablespoon pure maple syrup

Key Lime Filling
1 can (14 ounces/400 mL) full fat coconut milk

¼ cup pure maple syrup

2 tablespoons arrowroot flour

4 egg yolks

Zest and juice of 5 or 6 limes (about ½ cup lime juice)

½ large ripe avocado, pitted and peeled

Topping
1 batch Coconut Whip

Lime zest (optional)

These perfectly tart and naturally sweetened key lime pie puddings are baked and served in glass jars for easy sharing and eating. Lately I've been really into tart and sweet flavours combined, so this zesty lime-and-avocado-filled dessert definitely hits the spot. Grab your spoon and dig in to scoop up all those delicious flavours and layers in every bite. I use regular limes to keep things simple since they are easier to find and the recipe comes together faster.

1. Preheat the oven to 350°F.

2. **Make the Crust** In a food processor, combine the oats, pecans, coconut, cinnamon, and salt. Process for 1 minute. Add the coconut oil and maple syrup and process for 20 to 30 seconds until crumbly.

3. Divide the crust mixture among six 8-ounce wide mouth ovenproof glass jars. Press the crust into the bottom of each jar using your fingers or a wooden spoon if not using a wide mouth jar. Pierce the bottom with a fork. Put the jars on a small baking sheet and bake for 25 minutes, or until slightly golden.

4. **Make the Key Lime Filling** In a blender, combine the coconut milk, maple syrup, arrowroot flour, egg yolks, lime zest, lime juice, and avocado. Blend for 30 seconds. Pour into a medium saucepan and bring to a simmer over medium-high heat. Reduce the heat to medium-low and cook, whisking constantly, until the filling becomes thick and coats the back of a spoon, about 5 minutes. Divide the filling among the jars and let cool completely. Cover and refrigerate for 4 to 6 hours or overnight to set.

5. Serve chilled with a dollop of Coconut Whip and a sprinkle of lime zest, if using. Store any leftovers in the fridge for up to 4 days.

VARIATION Swap out the lime for lemon or blood orange for different flavours.

🥥 **HEALTHNUT TIP** Make sure you use full-fat coconut milk from a can, as other varieties, such as light canned coconut milk, or coconut milk from a carton, will not thicken up enough.

Date Pecan Butter Tarts

Makes 12 tarts • Prep Time 15 minutes • Bake Time 25 minutes

....

Prep Ahead
Spelt Pastry Dough (page 221)

Ingredients

2½ cups Medjool dates, pitted
   (about 25 dates)

1 batch Spelt Pastry Dough

3 tablespoons pure maple syrup,
   plus more for drizzling

4 teaspoons ghee or organic
   unsalted butter, melted

2 teaspoons pure vanilla extract

Sea salt

¾ cup unsalted raw pecans

A classic Canadian treat, pecan butter tarts are one dessert I've been dying to make a healthier version of for years. Instead of the traditional butter, sugar, and egg filling, I used the almighty Medjool date to give the tarts a rich, gooey, caramel-like texture that works so well with the flaky crust and nutty maple pecan topping. Pair these with your cup of Tim Hortons, and you have yourself an excellent day, eh?

1. Preheat the oven to 350°F.

2. In a small bowl, cover the dates with boiling water and let soak for 10 minutes.

3. Meanwhile, using your hands, knead the Spelt Pastry Dough into a ball. Divide the dough into 2 equal pieces. Wrap one piece in plastic wrap and return to the refrigerator. On a floured work surface, roll out the dough until ¼ inch thick. Using a 4-inch round cookie cutter, cut out 12 circles, rerolling the scraps if needed. Carefully press the circles into 12 muffin cups. You may need to stretch the dough a bit before placing it in the cups. Place the muffin tin in the fridge while you make the filling.

4. To make the date filling, drain the dates, reserving 1 tablespoon of the date water. In a food processor, combine the dates, maple syrup, ghee, vanilla, and a pinch of salt. Process for 1 minute. Add the date water and process for another 2 minutes.

5. Scoop a heaping tablespoon of date filling into each pastry shell and smooth the filling with the back of a spoon. Arrange 3 pecan halves on top of each tart and drizzle with maple syrup.

6. Bake for 25 minutes, or until the crust is golden brown and the filling is bubbling. Let the tarts cool in the pan for 10 minutes. Run a thin knife around the edges and lift out the tarts. Transfer to a rack to cool completely. Store any leftovers in an airtight container at room temperature for up to 2 days or in the fridge for up to 1 week.

Toasty Lemon Coconut Macaroons with Chocolate Drizzle

Makes 12 macaroons • **Prep Time 15 minutes** • **Bake Time 20 to 22 minutes**

Ingredients

4 cups unsweetened shredded
   coconut

2 egg whites

¼ teaspoon salt

3 tablespoons pure liquid honey

2 tablespoons coconut oil, melted

Zest of 1 lemon

1 tablespoon fresh lemon juice

1 teaspoon pure vanilla extract

½ cup semi-sweet chocolate chips
   (dairy-free, if required)

2 tablespoons coconut oil

These lemony nests of toasted coconut are a perfectly sweetened treat to enjoy after dinner or for a midday snack. The soft and chewy coconut inside combined with the crispy coconut outside, all dipped and drizzled in chocolate, makes me unable to resist eating a couple or five (who's counting?). Simple, delicate, and light, these puffs of coconut are just too good not to make several batches.

1. Preheat the oven to 325°F. Line a baking sheet with parchment paper.

2. Spread the shredded coconut on the baking sheet and lightly toast in the oven for 3 to 4 minutes.

3. In a medium bowl, combine the egg whites and salt and beat with a hand-held electric mixer for 3 to 4 minutes, until stiff white peaks form.

4. In a large bowl, whisk together the honey, coconut oil, lemon zest, lemon juice, and vanilla. Add the toasted coconut and stir until well coated. Gently fold in the egg whites until combined.

5. Scoop heaping tablespoons of the coconut mixture and drop onto the prepared baking sheet, spacing 1 inch apart. Bake for 20 to 22 minutes, until deep brown on the bottoms and golden brown on top. Transfer to a rack to cool completely. Set aside the lined baking sheet.

6. In a heatproof bowl set over (not in) a saucepan of simmering water, melt the chocolate chips with the coconut oil, stirring until smooth. Dip the bottoms of the macaroons in the chocolate and place on the lined baking sheet, then use a fork to drizzle chocolate over the top of the macaroons. Transfer to the fridge or freezer for 5 to 10 minutes, until the chocolate has hardened. Store in an airtight container at room temperature for up to 3 days.

VARIATION Drizzle Coconut Butter Lemon Glaze (page 232) over the macaroons instead of chocolate.

Cake Doughnuts

Makes 6 doughnuts • Prep Time 15 minutes • Bake Time 10 to 12 minutes

Prep Ahead

Coconut Butter Lemon Glaze
    (page 232)

Ingredients

1½ teaspoons apple cider vinegar

½ cup unsweetened soy milk

1¼ cups light spelt flour

1 teaspoon baking powder

½ teaspoon baking soda

¼ teaspoon salt

1 egg

½ cup coconut sugar

1 teaspoon pure vanilla extract

¼ cup coconut oil, melted

½ cup Coconut Butter Lemon Glaze

1 tablespoon grated red beet

Sprinkles, for decoration

HEALTHNUT TIP If you're not eating all the doughnuts right away, don't glaze the extras for easy storing. Store them unglazed in the fridge, then glaze and decorate them before serving so they are nice and fresh.

These sugary round rings of dough have become quite the food celebrity. I feel like there are just as many different doughnuts in the world as there are types of people! You can find them stuffed, with a hole, mini, round, dipped, rolled, twisted, powdered . . . the list goes on. My favourite when I was growing up was the classic honey dip, but I think my childhood self would even appreciate these soft and fluffy baked cake doughnuts with a pink glaze and sprinkles for crunch. Great for parties, as afternoon treats, or for dipping in your morning coffee.

1. Preheat the oven to 350°F. Lightly spray a 6-cavity doughnut pan with coconut oil.

2. In a measuring cup, stir the cider vinegar into the soy milk and set aside for about 5 minutes to curdle. This will create a non-dairy "buttermilk."

3. In a large bowl, combine the spelt flour, baking powder, baking soda, and salt. Give it a quick stir.

4. In a medium bowl, using a hand-held electric mixer, beat the egg, coconut sugar, and vanilla on medium speed for 30 seconds. Beat for another 10 seconds while slowly adding the coconut oil and the soy milk mixture. Add the egg mixture to the flour mixture and stir with a spatula just until combined; do not overmix.

5. Spoon the batter into the doughnut pan, filling each cavity about three-quarters full. Smooth the top of the batter with the back of a spoon or a spatula. Bake for 10 to 12 minutes, until a toothpick inserted in the centre comes out clean. Let the doughnuts cool in the pan on a rack for 10 minutes before turning them out on the rack to cool completely.

6. Put the Coconut Butter Lemon Glaze in a small shallow bowl. Wearing rubber gloves to prevent staining your hands, squeeze out 1 teaspoon of juice from the beet pulp. Add to the glaze and stir until the mixture is an even bright pink hue.

7. Dip the top of each cooled doughnut about halfway into the glaze, twisting slightly as you lift up to remove excess glaze. Place the doughnuts back on the rack, decorate with sprinkles, and let rest for 5 minutes so the glaze can set. Store in an airtight container at room temperature for up to 2 days or in the fridge for up to 5 days (see Tip).

Lemon Pie Chia Pudding

Serves 2 to 4 • Prep Time 5 minutes • Chill Time 30 minutes or overnight

....

Prep Ahead

Coconut Whip (page 231)

Ingredients

1 can (14 ounces/400 mL)
   full-fat coconut milk

3 tablespoons chia seeds

2 tablespoons pure maple syrup

1 teaspoon pure vanilla extract

½ teaspoon ground turmeric

Zest and juice of 1 lemon

Toppings

½ cup Coconut Whip

1 tablespoon toasted unsweetened
   coconut

Lemon zest (optional)

Honestly, what can't a chia seed do? Whether they're blended into smoothies, turned into an egg replacement, or, in this case, thickening a creamy dessert, chia seeds are a chameleon superfood. Lemony, tart, rich, and creamy, this lemon pie–inspired chia pudding gives me all the feels. You can now have that lemon pie experience in 30 minutes, with no baking necessary. And just to give it that traditional bright yellow hue we've grown up to love in our lemon pie, I've added a touch of turmeric for an extra pop of natural colour. This surprisingly healthy dessert will sweep you off your feet!

1. In a medium glass jar, combine the coconut milk, chia seeds, maple syrup, vanilla, turmeric, and lemon zest and juice. Cover and shake well to combine. Refrigerate for 30 minutes or overnight, stirring occasionally to prevent the chia seeds from clumping.

2. Divide the chia pudding among small bowls, top with Coconut Whip, and sprinkle with toasted coconut and lemon zest, if using. The chia pudding can be stored, without toppings, in an airtight container in the fridge for up to 5 days.

Peanut Butter Chocolate Cheesecake

Makes 12 squares • **Soak Time 4 to 6 hours or overnight** • **Prep Time 20 minutes** • **Chill Time 4 hours or overnight**

Filling

1½ cups raw cashews

¾ cup canned full-fat coconut milk

½ cup natural smooth peanut butter

¼ cup pure maple syrup

Juice of 1 lemon

2 tablespoons solid coconut oil

1 teaspoon pure vanilla extract

¼ teaspoon sea salt (omit if using
   salted peanut butter)

Crust

1 cup old-fashioned rolled oats

1 cup raw pecans

¼ teaspoon cinnamon

¼ teaspoon sea salt

1 cup Medjool dates
   (about 10 dates), pitted

2 tablespoons coconut oil, melted

Topping

¼ cup semi-sweet chocolate chips
   (dairy-free, if required)

1 tablespoon coconut oil

Chopped salted peanuts

VARIATION If you're serving this
at a party, you can make it in an
8-inch springform pan and serve
it cake style.

Peanut butter meets cheesecake with drizzled chocolate and crushed peanuts. It just doesn't get any better than this. The creamy, slightly tangy peanut butter cheesecake filling is poured over a chewy graham cracker–inspired crust made from pecans, dates, oats, and a little spice. Set it all in the freezer, add your toppings, and you have the ultimate chilled dessert, perfect for backyard barbecues, Friday girls' night, or solo Netflix-and-chill with a glass of wine.

1. Soak the cashews in enough water to cover for 4 to 6 hours or overnight.

2. **Make the Crust** In a food processor, combine the oats, pecans, cinnamon, and salt. Process for 15 seconds or until the mixture is a fine crumble. Add the dates and process until blended. With the machine running, slowly add the melted coconut oil, and process until the mixture sticks together when pressed between your fingers.

3. Grease an 8-inch square baking pan with coconut oil (it helps the parchment paper stick better) and line the pan with parchment paper, leaving an overhang at the sides. (This will make it easier to remove the bars after freezing.) Transfer the crust mixture to the pan and press it firmly and evenly onto the bottom. Place in the freezer to firm up while you make the filling.

4. **Make the Filling** Drain and rinse the cashews and transfer them to a high-speed blender. Add the coconut milk, peanut butter, maple syrup, lemon juice, coconut oil, vanilla, and salt, if using. Blend until smooth and silky. Pour the filling over the crust and smooth the top with a rubber spatula. Freeze for 4 hours or overnight, until set.

5. **Make the Topping** In a heatproof bowl set over (not in) a saucepan of simmering water, melt the chocolate with the coconut oil, stirring until smooth. Drizzle the chocolate over the frozen filling, then top with chopped peanuts. The chocolate will set quickly because of the frozen filling. Return to the freezer until ready to serve.

6. To serve, remove the cheesecake from the pan and let sit at room temperature for 5 to 10 minutes to soften slightly. Using a sharp knife that's been heated under hot water, slice into 12 squares. Store any leftovers in an airtight container in the freezer for up to 1 month.

Caramelized Bananas Foster Crepes

Serves 4 • **Prep Time 10 minutes** • **Cook Time 5 minutes**

Prep Ahead

Easy Blender Crepes (page 220)

Coconut Whip (231)

Ingredients

2 tablespoons ghee or organic
   unsalted butter

½ cup chopped raw walnuts

¼ cup pure maple syrup

1 teaspoon pure vanilla extract

½ teaspoon cinnamon

Sea salt

2 ripe medium bananas, sliced

1 batch Easy Blender Crepes

I batch Coconut Whip, for serving

Bananas caramelized in a buttery maple sauce, served on top of warm stacked crepes. When I was bartending at a trendy little bar in Perth, Australia, they used to serve bananas Foster panna cotta, and it quickly became one of my favourite flavours. Here's my spin! A simplified, no refined sugar version with banana and walnuts spiced with vanilla and cinnamon. Although this dessert originated in New Orleans, I'm thankful that its deliciousness has spread across the globe—and to the HealthNut kitchen.

1. In a large non-stick skillet, melt the ghee over medium heat. Add the walnuts, maple syrup, vanilla, cinnamon, and a pinch of salt. Reduce the heat to low and cook for 2 minutes, stirring constantly. Add the sliced bananas and cook for 1 minute, stirring constantly.

2. To assemble, on each plate, fold 2 crepes in half, then fold in half again. Spoon one-quarter of the warm banana caramel mixture over the 2 folded crepes and top with a dollop of Coconut Whip. Repeat with the remaining crepes, folded, and serve immediately.

Banana Soft Serve Four Ways

Serves 3 • **Prep Time 5 minutes**

Smooth, fruity, and so tasty you won't believe there's no added sugar or dairy in this "ice cream." I love that I can take the frozen peeled bananas that I use for my morning smoothies and make a creamy, dreamy ice-cream dessert! Mix and match the flavours, grab your cup or cone, and pop on a scoop of this delicious no-churn ice cream that's ready in minutes.

This banana soft serve is best served fresh, as it will start to melt quite quickly. Store any leftovers in an airtight container in the freezer for up to 2 weeks. If serving from frozen, let sit at room temperature for a few minutes for a soft serve consistency, otherwise it will be too solid to scoop.

Tropical Mango Lime

Ingredients

2 frozen ripe medium bananas, chopped

2 cups frozen mango chunks

Juice of 1 lime

⅓ to ½ cup canned full-fat coconut milk

½ teaspoon pure vanilla extract

1. In a high-speed blender, combine the bananas, mango, lime juice, coconut milk (start with ⅓ cup and add more if needed), and vanilla. Blend on high speed for 1 minute, or until smooth, stopping to scrape down the sides as needed.

Mint Chocolate Chip

Ingredients

3 frozen ripe medium bananas, chopped

1 cup frozen cubed ripe avocado

6 to 8 fresh mint leaves

⅓ to ½ cup canned full-fat coconut milk

½ teaspoon pure vanilla extract

½ teaspoon peppermint extract

¼ cup semi-sweet chocolate chips, roughly chopped

1. In a high-speed blender, combine the bananas, avocado, mint leaves, coconut milk (start with ⅓ cup and add more if needed), vanilla, and peppermint extract. Blend on high speed for 1 minute, or until smooth, stopping to scrape down the sides as needed. Add the chopped chocolate chips and pulse for 5 seconds.

recipe continues

Peach Raspberry

Ingredients

2 frozen ripe medium bananas,
   chopped

1 cup frozen sliced peaches

1 cup frozen raspberries

Juice of ½ orange

⅓ to ½ cup canned full-fat
   coconut milk

½ teaspoon pure vanilla extract

1. In a high-speed blender, combine the bananas, peaches, raspberries, orange juice, coconut milk (start with ⅓ cup and add more if needed), and vanilla. Blend on high speed for 1 minute, or until smooth, stopping to scrape down the sides as needed.

Chocolate Chip Cookie Dough

Prep Ahead

Raw Chocolate Chip Cookie Dough
   Bites (page 189)

Ingredients

4 frozen ripe medium bananas,
   chopped

⅓ to ½ cup canned full-fat
   coconut milk

1 teaspoon pure vanilla extract

Sea salt

4 Raw Chocolate Chip Cookie
   Dough Bites

1. In a high-speed blender, combine the bananas, coconut milk (start with ⅓ cup and add more if needed), vanilla, and a pinch of salt. Blend on high speed for 2 to 3 minutes, until smooth, stopping to scrape down the sides as needed. Crumble in the Raw Chocolate Chip Cookie Dough Bites and pulse for 5 seconds.

HEALTHNUT TIP Best when made in a high-speed blender and using a tamper. You can also use a food processor, but it will take a little bit more time (stopping and scraping the sides) and liquid to get to that creamy ice-cream consistency.

HEALTHNUT
STAPLES

Eggs Four Ways

Boiled, poached, scrambled, sunny-side-up, whichever way you crack it, eggs are one of the best staple foods. They are a convenient protein-packed ingredient to have stocked in your fridge at all times for baking, breakfast, or—my favourite—quick lunches. Here are four of my go-to ways to cook eggs. You'll find these scattered throughout the book, such as in Gigi's Warm Black-Eyed Pea Salad (page 117) or Sunday Brunch Bowl (page 46). Use this as your how-to guide for cooking the perfect egg every time.

Poached Eggs   Serves 2 • Cook Time 3 minutes

Ingredients
1 tablespoon apple cider vinegar
Sea salt
2 eggs
Pepper

🌰 **HEALTHNUT TIP** For best results, make sure your eggs are fresh, as they tend to be less watery and the whites stay together better. Test them by placing them in a bowl of cold water. If the egg sinks to the bottom, it's fresh. If it floats, toss it.

1. Pour a couple of inches of water into a medium saucepan and bring to a simmer over medium heat. Whisk in the cider vinegar and a pinch of sea salt.

2. Crack 1 egg into a small bowl. Using a butter knife, stir the water to create a swirl and then slowly slide the egg into the water. Wait 30 to 60 seconds for the egg whites to cook and turn slightly white and then gently swirl the water next to the first egg before adding the second egg. Cook each egg for about 3 minutes for a runny yolk. Gently remove the poached egg using a slotted spoon, tap off excess water, transfer to a plate, and season with salt and pepper.

Fluffy Scrambled Eggs   Serves 2 • Prep Time 2 minutes • Cook Time 5 minutes

Ingredients
4 eggs
2 tablespoons unsweetened almond milk or soy milk
Sea salt and pepper
1 teaspoon ghee or organic unsalted butter

🌰 **HEALTHNUT TIP** Low and slow is the best practice for the ultimate fluffy scrambled eggs.

1. In a small bowl, combine the eggs with the almond milk and a pinch each of salt and pepper. Whisk until the yolks and whites are fully combined.

2. In a medium non-stick skillet, melt the ghee over medium-low heat. Pour in the whisked eggs and let sit and cook for 1 minute.

3. Run a rubber spatula around the edges and push the eggs towards the middle of the pan to create pillowy folds while cooking for another 2 to 3 minutes until no longer runny, lowering the heat if necessary to prevent the eggs from drying out. Remove from the heat while the eggs are still glossy and slightly wet; they will continue to cook in the hot pan.

4. With the spatula, break up the scrambled eggs into large chunks. Serve warm.

recipe continues

Sunny-Side-Up Eggs   Serves 2 • Cook Time 3 to 4 minutes

Ingredients

2 teaspoons avocado oil or
   extra-virgin olive oil

4 eggs

Sea salt and pepper

1. Heat the avocado oil in a medium non-stick skillet over medium-high heat. Carefully crack the eggs into the skillet, leaving space between each egg. Cook for 3 to 4 minutes, or until the whites are cooked and no longer translucent and the yolks are still runny. Sprinkle with a pinch each of salt and pepper. Serve immediately.

🌰 **HEALTHNUT TIP** If your egg whites aren't setting quickly enough, you can cover the pan with a lid or spoon some of the hot oil on top of the white.

Jammy Eggs   Serves 2 • Cook Time 7 minutes

Ingredients

Salt

4 eggs

1. Fill a medium saucepan with water, add a pinch of salt, and bring to a boil over medium-high heat. With a slotted spoon, gently lower the eggs into the pan and cook for 7 minutes. Transfer to a bowl of ice water and chill for 2 minutes.

2. Remove from the water and with the back of a spoon gently tap the shell to crack it. Peel the eggs and serve warm.

🌰 **HEALTHNUT TIP** Timing is everything! Set a timer for exactly 7 minutes so you get the perfect jammy result every time.

Fluffy Cooked Quinoa

Makes 3 cups • Cook Time 12 to 15 minutes

Ingredients

1 cup dry quinoa

2 cups water

Sea salt

Is it a seed, is it a grain? It's super quinoa! Technically, quinoa is a seed, but it cooks up just like a grain and can be enjoyed hot or cold for a protein-packed, gluten-free alternative to rice or grain. Throughout this book you will see how often I use it: as a base in my Farmers' Market Bowl (page 151), as a batter in my Baked Crispy Quinoa Chicken Fingers (page 180), and for breakfast in my Almond Orange Quinoa Oatmeal (page 33). Pronounced keen-wah, this amazing karaoke-sounding food needs to be a staple in every pantry.

1. In a medium saucepan, combine the quinoa, water, and a pinch of salt. Stir and bring to a boil. Reduce the heat to low, cover, and simmer for 12 to 15 minutes, until the quinoa is tender and the water is absorbed. Remove from the heat and let sit, covered, for another 3 to 5 minutes. Fluff with a fork and enjoy warm or chilled.

COOKING QUINOA

DRY QUINOA	WATER	COOKED QUINOA
¼ cup	½ cup	¾ cup
⅓ cup	⅔ cup	1 cup
⅔ cup	1⅓ cup	2 cups
1 cup	2 cups	3 cups

VARIATION If you want more flavour, you can cook the quinoa in low-sodium chicken or vegetable stock instead.

Easy Blender Crepes

Makes 8 medium crepes • Prep Time 15 minutes • Cook Time 10 minutes

Ingredients

2 eggs

1 cup unsweetened almond milk
   or soy milk

1 cup brown rice flour

1 tablespoon pure liquid honey

Sea salt

There's this little crepe place at my local mall that makes the best French crepes. I never realized how simple they were to make, and how versatile they are, until I tried making them on my own. My version is gluten- and dairy-free, but I assure you they are just as good as the classic: soft, tender, and just slightly sweet. Enjoy them savoury in my Eggs Benny on a Crepe (page 57) or sweet in my Caramelized Bananas Foster Crepes (page 210).

1. In a blender, combine the eggs, almond milk, brown rice flour, honey, and a pinch of salt. Blend for 10 to 15 seconds until just smooth. Try not to overblend. Let the batter sit for 10 minutes to thicken.

2. Preheat the oven to 200°F.

3. Heat a medium non-stick skillet over medium-low heat and spray with a light coating of coconut oil. Add ¼ cup of batter and gently swirl the pan so the batter evenly coats the bottom (crepes should be around 6-inch circles). Cook for 1 to 2 minutes, until the edges are dry and the top appears slightly bubbly. Run a thin rubber spatula around the edges of the crepe, then carefully flip and cook for another 30 seconds. Transfer to a casserole dish with a lid and keep warm in the oven while you cook the remaining crepes.

4. Cool leftover crepes completely before transferring to a resealable freezer bag, removing all the air before sealing. Store in the fridge for up to 5 days or in the freezer for up to 1 month.

VARIATION Use buckwheat flour instead of brown rice flour.

Spelt Pastry Dough

Makes 1 batch of dough • Prep Time 5 minutes

Ingredients

1½ cups light spelt flour

½ teaspoon sea salt

½ cup chilled cubed,
   organic unsalted butter

3 tablespoons ice water

This dough is going to become your go-to staple when making anything from my Spring Veggie Quiche Tarts (page 170) to my Strawberry Rhubarb Hand Pies (page 196). It will not let you down! The best part is that it comes together in less than 5 minutes in a food processor. All you need is flour, salt, water, and butter.

1. In a food processor, process the spelt flour and salt for 5 seconds. Add the butter and process for 10 to 15 seconds, until a fine crumble. With the machine running, add the water 1 tablespoon at a time, processing for 15 seconds until the dough forms a ball.

2. Use immediately, or tightly wrap in plastic wrap and store in an airtight container in the fridge for up to 3 days, or shape into a thick disc (this will make rolling out easier once the butter has hardened) and freeze for up to 1 month. If frozen, allow to thaw in the fridge (not at room temperature) overnight before using.

VARIATION For a dairy-free version, swap out the butter for the same amount of cubed cold coconut oil. This dough will be a bit more delicate, so you'll need to roll it out between 2 pieces of parchment paper, or it will stick to your rolling pin or break.

 **HEALTHNUT TIP** You can easily double this recipe in the food processor to make multiple batches of dough at the same time.

Crispy Oven Bacon

Makes 1 pound cooked bacon • Prep Time 2 minutes • Cook Time 15 minutes

Ingredients
1 pound (450 g) thick-cut bacon

The world may not agree on whether bacon is healthy or not, but I don't think anyone can deny that it's pretty darn tasty. I don't make it part of my everyday diet, but when I do want to enjoy it, I buy the best quality I can get my hands on, usually from the farmers' market. Save time and avoid cleaning up messy oil splatters by using this easy oven bacon hack that gives you perfectly crispy (and mess-free) bacon every time.

1. Preheat the oven to 400°F. Line a baking sheet with parchment paper.

2. Spread the bacon strips evenly on the baking sheet. Bake for 10 minutes. Turn and bake for another 5 minutes, or until desired crispness.

3. Transfer to a plate lined with paper towel to drain.

🌰 **HEALTHNUT TIP** Look for good-quality bacon. Avoid additives and ingredients like refined sugar and nitrates.

Steamed and Frozen Veggies for Smoothies

Steamed and frozen vegetables such as butternut squash and cauliflower are my secret weapon for adding a creamy frozen texture to my smoothies without having to use loads of bananas or other fruit. Don't get me wrong, I'm not anti-fruit by any means, but I like to keep my smoothies balanced with a fairly equal mix of fruits and veggies. It's a great way to get a variety of vitamins and nutrients into my meals. Instead of relying on the same bases for your smoothies all the time, try switching things up. You'll be pleasantly surprised by how thick and delicious your morning liquid breakfast will taste—and you'll get in some extra servings of veggies!

Steamed and Frozen Cauliflower Florets   **Prep Time 5 minutes** • **Cook Time 5 to 7 minutes**

Ingredients
1 head cauliflower

🌰 **HEALTHNUT TIP** For a quick hack, transfer the cooled cauliflower in a single layer to a large freezer bag. Keep the bag horizontal and place in the freezer.

1. Remove the stem, cut the cauliflower into florets, and give them a quick rinse.

2. Pour 2 inches of water into a large pot, add a steamer basket, and bring to a boil. Reduce the heat to medium, add the cauliflower, and cover the pot. Steam for 5 to 7 minutes, until lightly steamed but still firm.

3. Transfer to a parchment-lined baking sheet and let cool completely. Place the tray of cauliflower in the freezer for 1 to 2 hours.

4. Transfer the cauliflower to a resealable freezer bag and store in the freezer for up to 3 months.

Steamed and Frozen Butternut Squash   **Prep Time 5 minutes** • **Cook Time 7 to 9 minutes**

Ingredients
1 butternut squash

🌰 **HEALTHNUT TIP** If you are short on time, you can buy already peeled and chopped butternut squash ready to be steamed, roasted, or boiled into soups.

1. Trim ends from the squash and peel using a strong vegetable peeler. Using a sharp knife, cut the squash in half lengthwise and scoop out the seeds and pulp with a large spoon. Cut the squash into 1-inch cubes.

2. Pour 2 inches of water into a large pot, add a steamer basket, and bring to a boil. Reduce the heat to medium, add the butternut squash, and cover the pot. Steam for 7 to 9 minutes, until the squash is fork-tender but still firm.

3. Transfer to a parchment-lined baking sheet and allow to cool completely. Place the tray of butternut squash in the freezer and freeze for 1 to 2 hours.

4. Transfer the squash to a resealable freezer bag and store in the freezer for up to 3 months.

Quick Pickled Red Onions

Makes 1 cup • **Prep Time 5 minutes**

Ingredients

1 red onion

1 clove garlic, thinly sliced

½ cup apple cider vinegar

1 tablespoon pure liquid honey
   or pure maple syrup

1 teaspoon black peppercorns

½ teaspoon sea salt

1 to 2 cups water

Sweet and sour, these bright pink pickled onions are incredibly flavourful and add a pretty pop of colour to any appetizer, burger, taco, sandwich, or nacho plate. Whatever you sneak them into, you'll love the burst of tang and crunch they add to your food. Try them in my Cheesy Bean Loaded Nachos (page 87).

1. Peel the onion and cut into ¼-inch slices. Separate the rings and place in a medium bowl. Cover with boiling water and let sit for 3 minutes.

2. Drain the onions. In a 16-ounce glass jar, combine the garlic, cider vinegar, honey, peppercorns, and salt. Cover and shake. Add the onion rings to the vinegar mixture, top with enough water to submerge the onions, and cover with the lid. Refrigerate for 30 minutes for a quick pickle or for 4 to 6 hours for a deeper flavour. Store any leftovers in the fridge for up to 2 weeks.

Almond Flour Parm

Makes 1 cup • **Prep Time 5 minutes**

Ingredients

1 cup almond flour

2 tablespoons nutritional yeast

1 teaspoon sea salt

½ teaspoon garlic powder

2 teaspoons extra-virgin olive oil

I thought up this clever idea while baking with almond flour one day and realizing how much the consistency of the flour reminded me of Parmesan cheese. So I added a few spices and seasoning and—ta-da!— the easiest parm you've ever made! Sprinkle it on everything and anything, from kale chips and avocado toast, to my Mushroom Fettuccine Alfredo (page 155) and Easy Peasy Pesto Pasta (page 156).

1. In a small food processor, combine the almond flour, nutritional yeast, salt, and garlic powder. Process for about 5 seconds to combine. Add the olive oil and process for another 5 to 7 seconds until the oil is well distributed. Store in an airtight container in the fridge for up to 2 weeks.

🌰 **HEALTHNUT TIP** If you don't have almond flour on hand, grind some blanched almonds in a food processor for 10 seconds as a quick almond flour hack.

Nacho Average Cheese Sauce

Makes 1¼ cups • **Soak Time 4 to 6 hours or overnight** • **Prep Time 5 minutes** • **Cook Time 15 minutes**

Ingredients

¼ cup raw cashews

1 small sweet potato, peeled and cut into ½-inch cubes

¾ cup unsweetened almond milk or soy milk

Juice of ½ lemon

2 tablespoons nutritional yeast

1 tablespoon white miso

1 teaspoon onion powder

1 teaspoon garlic powder

1 teaspoon arrowroot flour

1 teaspoon gluten-free tamari

¼ teaspoon ground turmeric

¼ teaspoon smoked paprika

Cayenne pepper

Sea salt

Get your nacho fix and a side of veggies with this cheese-less but flavourful nacho cheese sauce. This stuff brings me right back to ordering tortilla chips, salsa, and nacho cheese at amusement parks when I was a kid. I have to admit, it is still one of my guilty pleasures. This cheesy, silky nacho cheese sauce will fool your taste buds into thinking you're eating the real deal but with hidden sweet potato and cashews. Drizzle this on Cheesy Bean Loaded Nachos (page 87), mix it into Baked Mac and Cheese, Please (page 159), or just give in and eat it with a spoon, because it's basically soup . . . right? I love making this the day before so the flavours have time to intensify.

1. Soak the cashews in enough water to cover for 4 to 6 hours or overnight. Drain and rinse before using.

2. Pour 2 inches of water into a large pot with a steamer basket and bring to a boil. Put the sweet potatoes in a steamer basket, cover, and steam for 10 minutes, or until fork-tender.

3. In a blender, combine the sweet potatoes, cashews, almond milk, lemon juice, nutritional yeast, miso, onion powder, garlic powder, arrowroot, tamari, turmeric, paprika, and a pinch each of cayenne and salt. Blend for 1 minute, or until smooth.

4. Pour the sauce into a medium saucepan and bring to a simmer over medium-high heat. Reduce the heat to medium and cook for 5 minutes, whisking constantly.

5. Serve immediately. Store any leftovers in an airtight container in the fridge for up to 5 days or in the freezer for up to 1 month.

🌰 **HEALTHNUT TIP** This sauce freezes and reheats well. You might need to add a splash of milk to thin it out a bit when reheating on the stovetop.

Easy Peasy Pesto

Makes ¾ cup • Prep Time 5 minutes

Ingredients

1 cup loosely packed fresh
  basil leaves

½ cup fresh mint leaves

¼ cup fresh or thawed
  frozen green peas

¼ cup pine nuts

¼ cup extra-virgin olive oil

2 tablespoons fresh lemon juice

2 cloves garlic, chopped

¼ teaspoon sea salt

Pepper

Sure, you can buy pesto, but it just doesn't compare to homemade. This simple and fresh basil, mint, and green pea version—the perfect combination of nutty, garlicky, and lemony—can be mixed into a plate of my Easy Peasy Pesto Pasta (page 156), spread on some crackers, or tossed with steamed veggies.

1. In a small food processor, combine the basil, mint, peas, pine nuts, olive oil, lemon juice, garlic, salt, and a pinch of pepper. Process for 30 seconds or until a textured paste forms, stopping to scrape down the sides halfway through.

2. Store in an airtight container in the fridge for up to 4 days or in the freezer for up to 1 month.

VARIATION Pine nuts can be pricey, but you can swap them out for walnuts or cashews for a similar buttery and nutty texture and flavour.

HEALTHNUT TIP Extend the life of your fresh herbs by storing them in a glass jar with 1 inch of water, covered loosely with a recycled produce or freezer bag to keep them fresh and wilt-free for up to 2 weeks. Some herbs, such as cilantro, thrive in a cooler temperature, so they are best stored in the fridge. Others, such as basil, are better suited for room-temperature storage on the kitchen counter.

Vanilla Roasted Almond Butter

Makes 1¼ cups • Prep Time 10 to 25 minutes • Bake Time 10 minutes

Ingredients

2 cups raw almonds

1 tablespoon coconut oil

1 teaspoon pure vanilla extract

1 teaspoon pure maple syrup
  (optional)

¼ teaspoon sea salt

Although grinding nuts into butter might sound like intimidating labour, it's actually quite easy. Most store-bought nut butters contain added sugars, table salt, and binders to make them spreadable and preservatives so they last longer on the shelf—ingredients that I don't want in my sandwich. This roasted almond butter, with a hint of vanilla, and maple syrup if you want it more dessert-like, is one condiment you can feel good about spreading on your morning toast or in my Almond Swirl Chocolate Brownies (page 193).

1. Preheat the oven to 350°F. Line a baking sheet with parchment paper.

2. Spread the almonds in a single layer on the baking sheet and roast for 10 minutes, stirring halfway through.

3. Transfer the almonds to a food processor. Add the coconut oil, vanilla, maple syrup (if using), and salt. Process for 10 to 20 minutes, until smooth and drippy, stopping frequently to scrape down the sides. Depending on the power of your food processor, the processing time may vary.

4. Store in a glass jar in the fridge for up to 1 month.

🌰 **HEALTHNUT TIP** Be patient and let your food processor do its magic. Just when you think nothing is going to happen, those ground nuts turn into creamy, silky buttah!

Avocado Ranch Dip

Makes ½ cup • Prep Time 5 minutes

. . . .

Ingredients

1 medium ripe avocado, pitted
    and peeled

¼ cup plain full-fat yogurt or
    coconut yogurt

1 tablespoon unsweetened almond
    milk or soy milk

1½ teaspoons apple cider vinegar

1 teaspoon onion powder

1 teaspoon garlic powder

1 teaspoon dried dill

½ teaspoon dried parsley

¼ teaspoon sea salt

¼ teaspoon pepper

Who doesn't love a good herb sauce to dip veggies into? This yummy, tangy ranch dip can easily be doubled or tripled for parties and is perfect as a spread, dressing, or good old-fashioned dip for your carrot and celery sticks. You'll find it spread onto my Southwest Black-Eyed Pea Burgers (page 145) and Chicken Crunch Wrap with Ranch (page 182).

1. In a small food processor, combine the avocado, yogurt, milk, cider vinegar, onion powder, garlic powder, dill, parsley, salt, and pepper. Process for 10 to 15 seconds, until smooth and thick.

2. Transfer to a small bowl and serve immediately or chill in the fridge for 1 to 2 hours. Store any leftovers in an airtight container in the fridge for up to 4 days.

VARIATION   This recipe also works well with lemon juice in place of apple cider vinegar to give it a nice citrus tang.

Maple Tahini Dressing

Makes ½ cup • **Prep Time 5 minutes**

Ingredients

½ cup water

¼ cup tahini

Juice of ½ lemon

1 tablespoon apple cider vinegar

1 tablespoon pure maple syrup

1 clove garlic, chopped

Sea salt and pepper

This is one of my favourite dressings, and one you'll find in many recipes throughout the book, such as in my Rainbow Chopped Salad (page 118) and drizzled over my Falafel Mediterranean Bowl (page 148). It's creamy, garlicky, and lemony, with a hint of sweetness from the maple syrup. This well-rounded dressing hits all the flavour notes and is so versatile— whether it's tossed in salads or used as a dip for summer rolls, it will not disappoint.

1. In a high-speed blender, combine the water, tahini, lemon juice, cider vinegar, maple syrup, garlic, and a pinch each of salt and pepper. Blend on high speed for 30 seconds, or until smooth, adding more water if needed depending on how thick your tahini is.

2. Use right away or store in a glass jar in the fridge for up to 5 days.

🌰 **HEALTHNUT TIP** When refrigerated the fats will thicken up, so you may need to thin out the dressing with some water until it's drippy again.

Coconut Whip

Makes 2 cups • Prep Time 5 minutes

Ingredients

1 can (14 ounces/400 mL) full-fat
coconut milk, refrigerated
overnight
1 tablespoon pure maple syrup
½ teaspoon pure vanilla extract

Whisked coconut cream made with three simple ingredients makes for the most fluffy topping. Use it just like traditional whipped cream! It's dreamy on Key Lime Pie in a Jar (page 199), Caramelized Bananas Foster Crepes (page 210), or dolloped on a mug of hot chocolate. If coconut flavour isn't your thing—don't worry, we can still be friends—you will be happy to hear that with the splash of vanilla and maple syrup, all you can taste is rich, creamy goodness.

1. Without shaking the can, open the can of coconut milk, scoop out the solid coconut cream, and transfer it to a chilled medium bowl. (Save the coconut water to use in smoothies.)

2. Using a hand-held electric mixer, beat the coconut cream on medium speed for 2 to 3 minutes, until light and fluffy, scraping down the sides from time to time. Add the maple syrup and vanilla and beat on high speed for an additional minute.

3. Use right away or store in an airtight container in the fridge for up to 1 week. It will firm up, so whisk it briefly before using.

VARIATION For a chocolate version, add 1 tablespoon of cacao powder. Perfect for icing cakes, or as a dip for fruit.

🌰 **HEALTHNUT TIP** I like to keep a couple of cans of coconut milk in the back of my fridge at all times, so I'm always prepared when dessert calls for a dollop of whipped "cream."

Coconut Butter Lemon Glaze

Makes ½ cup • **Prep Time 5 minutes**

Ingredients

¼ cup coconut butter, softened

2 tablespoons fresh lemon juice

2 tablespoons pure liquid honey

2 tablespoons unsweetened almond
  milk or soy milk

½ teaspoon pure vanilla extract

This is the best glaze I've ever made, and it looks just like the real deal but without the icing sugar. I would eat this stuff by the spoonful if it was socially acceptable. This glaze makes an appearance in many of my recipes, like my Lemon-Glazed Blueberry Muffins (page 190), Cake Doughnuts (page 204), and Strawberry Rhubarb Hand Pies (page 196). You can pretty much dip or drizzle anything, because it's just that good!

1. In a small bowl, whisk together the coconut butter, lemon juice, honey, almond milk, and vanilla until silky smooth.

2. Use right away or store in an airtight container in the fridge for up to 1 week.

VARIATION You can dye this glaze different colours using real food, such as beet juice for pink, turmeric powder for yellow, spirulina for green—get creative!

HEALTHNUT TIP If your coconut butter is solid and the oil has separated, place the jar with the lid on in a bowl of hot water for 10 to 15 minutes, stirring every 5 minutes until the butter is a creamy consistency.

Salted Caramel Butter

Makes ½ cup • **Prep Time 5 minutes** • **Cook Time 5 minutes**

Ingredients

¼ cup coconut oil

¼ cup brown rice syrup

2 tablespoons natural almond butter

½ teaspoon sea salt (use ¼ teaspoon
   if using salted almond butter)

Salted caramel anything is amazing, but often full of processed sugars and weird oils. I've created a healthier version using brown rice syrup for its sweet yet sticky caramel-like texture, and almond butter to make it all smooth and drippy. Great as a dip for sliced fruit, drizzled over pancakes or oatmeal, or in recipes like my Salted Caramel Stovetop Granola (page 41).

1. Melt the coconut oil, brown rice syrup, almond butter, and salt in a small saucepan over medium heat, whisking constantly until the mixture simmers. Reduce the heat to low and whisk for 30 seconds.

2. Remove from the heat and continue to stir for another 30 to 40 seconds, until the caramel is thick enough to coat the back of a spoon or drips in ribbon-like folds when you lift the whisk.

3. Store in a glass jar in the fridge for up to 2 weeks. When ready to use, whisk over low heat until the sauce is warm and drippy.

HEALTHNUT TIP If you're not a huge coconut oil fan because of the flavour, buy refined coconut oil, which has been slightly processed and doesn't have a coconutty flavour. It can also be a good choice for adding to recipes where you don't want a noticeable coconut taste.

Acknowledgements

To the village it took to bring this book to life! Go, book team!

When I was first approached to write this book, I had recently left my marketing job and had only been full-time with HealthNut Nutrition for a couple of months. It was a really scary time, filled with lots of fear and doubt about whether this was the right path for me. I don't know if it's a coincidence or fate, but I'm so thankful that the opportunity came to me just when I needed a sign from the universe that I had made the right choice. To me this book represents so much more than healthy recipes and written words on paper. It represents a fulfilled dream of one day writing a cookbook, and years of building an amazing online audience—the HealthNut Family—that is responsible for getting me to where I am today.

My Viewers To each and every person who has stumbled upon my blog, YouTube channel, or Instagram or Pinterest feeds, thank you for supporting me and allowing me to have the best job a girl could ever ask for (and more online friends than my teenage self could ever dream of). Thank you a million avocado emojis and more for picking up a copy of this book. I hope it helps inspire and motivate you to live your best life while eating healthy foods that look as good as they taste.

My Other Half, Mr. Matt To my best friend, roommate, and business partner who I've been lucky to call my boyfriend for over ten years now. Matt was here from the very beginning, believing in me when I knew nothing about starting a business, setting up a blog, or filming a YouTube video. Without you I honestly don't know if HealthNut Nutrition would even be here today. Although some may only see you behind the scenes, to me you have always been my right-hand advisor, supporter, and cheerleader. Thank you for the countless runs to the grocery store trying to figure out if cilantro and coriander are the same thing, and ranting about why on earth so many foods have multiple names. Thank you for reminding me to take a deep breath when I feel overwhelmed and in need of a bear hug. Thank you for doing all the business things I hate, like organizing hundreds of receipts for taxes that I stuffed into a shoebox, and for never letting my fears and anxieties get the best of me. Most of all, thank you for making me happy and excited about life and truly living the dream.

My Familia First and foremost, thank you to my beautiful mom, Grace, who is one of my biggest inspirations in life. Thank you for raising me to be the woman I am today. Thank you to my second mom, Tia Cris, who has always made me feel so loved and has encouraged me to be a strong, independent woman. Thank you to my little sister Cloe for being my very first employee and proving that sisters can work together and not kill each other . . . most of the time. Thank you to my cousin Caitlin for forever being an inspiration and lending a helping hand whenever needed—like proofreading my manuscript and laughing at my corny puns. Lastly, thank you to the woman who created all these amazing ladies, my Vovó Berta, for teaching me that food is something that brings family together and is meant to be enjoyed.

My Friends Thank you to my best friend since grade sixth, Yvonne, who is the most amazing friend you could ever ask for and one I can count on for anything. She has known me and put up with me through many stages in my life, but most important, she reminds me to be spontaneous, grateful, and grounded. And thank you to my dear friend Andrea, for hanging out in my kitchen for countless hours helping me transcribe my recipes onto paper and using your handy ruler app to see if the chicken strips are 1 inch or 1½ inches long (and proving that there really is an app for everything).

My Publishing Team Thank you, Andrea Magyar at Penguin Random House Canada, for believing in me and reaching out when I needed this the most. You have an incredible eye for what you do, and you truly live the life you promote through the books you help publish. Also, a huge thank you to Dan Ambrosio and the team at Da Capo for partnering with me on this book in the United States.

My Book Agent Rick Broadhead, you have been such a huge stepping stone throughout this whole process. In a world that was very new to me, you helped pave the way and provide both knowledge and guidance where I needed it the most.

My Photography Team When I first met photographer Kyla on a shoot, I knew I had met my future cookbook photographer. Thank you for bringing my recipes to life by marrying my love for food and colours in the best and tastiest way possible. Houston, thank you for pushing us through shooting eight recipes a day and being the strong leader and cook that you are. Also, a huge thank you to Madison and Craig from Lea Wood Company, who created the most beautiful custom wood, concrete, and coloured boards used in the photographs.

My Network, Kin Community To the beautiful and very fashionably dressed Kin team, you truly have been a key component to taking my business full-time and allowing me to stay true to my brand. Rick, Ashley, Maureen, Jenny, Morgan, Aimee, and the other amazing ladies have been the best team to work with and inspire me every day. Thank you for your persistence and determination.

My Internet Friends Growing a business in a field where there is no how-to-guide means that one of the most valuable resources is other bloggers and YouTubers I may have met online but are now real friends. Thank you to my friend and teacher Davida, who taught me to know my worth and for being my unofficial business mentor when going full-time. Thank you to one of my first inspirations for starting my blog, Joy, who taught me that I could turn my passion into a career online. And to so many more who have influenced me in myriad ways, know that I am grateful our paths crossed.

My Recipe Testers Thank you from the bottom of my heart to Alex, Erica, Hannah, Janelle, Jessica, Kira, and Leigh for donating your precious time and kitchens to testing countless recipes for this book to ensure they were perfect, with just the right amount of salt and pepper! Thank you for being rock stars and contributing to this book with a labour of love and food.

Index